MEDALS AND DECORATIONS

MEDALS AND DECORATIONS

Ian Angus

St. Martin's Press
New York

ACKNOWLEDGEMENTS

The author and publishers would like to thank the following for the use of illustrative material in this book.

Apsley House, Christie Manson & Wood, Government of India Tourist Office, Imperial War Museum, Israeli Government Tourist Centre, Japanese Information Centre, Mr James Mackay, Mary Evans Picture Library, National Army Museum, National Maritime Museum, National Portrait Gallery, Royal Humane Society, Society for Cultural Relations with the U.S.S.R., Sotheby & Co., Spink & Son, U.S.A. Embassy, Victoria and Albert Museum.

The Battle of Waterloo drawn by J C Stadler showing action around Quatre Bras farm house

Library of Congress Cataloging in Publication Data

Angus, Ian.
    Medals and Decorations.
    Includes index.
    1. Medals—History.   2. Medals—Collectors and collecting.   3. Decorations of honor.   I. Title.
CJ5539.A53   1975   737.2   74–33904

CONTENTS

Illustrations of medals and decorations are two thirds of actual size throughout, unless otherwise stated

1
THE ORIGIN OF MEDALS

Medals come in all shapes, sizes and metals, but basically they all stem from the same original idea of a form of personal decoration which was intended as a mark of favour or as a reward for services rendered. At a very early date, however, it became customary to strike medals which were not intended for wear and were meant to commemorate persons and events. These commemorative medals can usually, though not always, be distinguished from awarded medals by the fact that they do not have a ring or suspension bar attached to them. Commemorative medals form a large group in themselves and are coming back into fashion though not yet attaining the popularity they enjoyed with collectors before the First World War. The other kinds of medals have long been popular on account of their association with people who fought in wars and campaigns, who perhaps distinguished themselves on the field of battle or performed individual acts of heroism. Other medals were awarded to people for outstanding services, or as prizes, and these also possess a strong human interest for the story lying behind the award. And then there are the badges and insignia of the orders of chivalry. Many of these orders, like the Bath, the Garter and the Golden Fleece, are as ancient as they are quaintly named and to have belonged to such exclusive orders of knighthood has long been regarded as a high honour.

But where did it all begin? There are frequent references in the literature of Ancient Greece to the awards of arms and armour to the heroes and victors in war. A crown of laurel leaves was a symbolic way of recognising the achievements of generals and statesmen, and to this day many medals and decorations include a laurel wreath in their design. Both the Egyptians and the Romans struck plaques in bronze, silver or gold and awarded them to soldiers for bravery on the battlefield. These plaques were often added to the standards of the century or regiment, or were sometimes attached to the harness of horses, in much the same way as horse brasses are still used.

The earliest reference to something similar to the medals of the present day occurs in *Antiquities of the Jews* where the historian Josephus describes how King Alexander, in the third century B.C., was well pleased with Jonathan, the High Priest, and sent him a gold button as a mark of favour for his skill in leading the Jews in battle. Later Jonathan received a second gold button for his valour in the field of battle. The award of badges, pendants and jewels continued on an individual basis at sporadic intervals in Europe until fairly modern times. The campaign medal as we know it today is a nineteenth century invention, though it had many forerunners.

Commemorative medals, in the form of large coins, existed in Greek and Roman times, but virtually disappeared until the middle of the fifteenth century when there was a revival of this art in Italy. Most commemorative medals were cast in moulds and were therefore limited to a very small quantity. In the sixteenth century, however, medals were increasingly produced by striking from specially engraved hammers and anvils, in the same way as coins, and this meant that many more could be produced. Coinciding with the growth of struck commemorative medals came the medals struck for military services.

The first medals produced in recognition of military service were cast in limited quantities and were made in gold or silver after the defeat of the Spanish Armada in 1588. These medals were given to naval officers and important government officials by Queen Elizabeth, partly in recognition of services rendered and partly to celebrate the defeat of Spain. The obverse (or 'heads' side) bears a very flattering portrait of Good Queen

left A medieval woodcut of knights on a quest and their adventures. The stories inspired the founding of many chivalric orders

The Armada panel shows the battle off Gravesend which prevented the Spaniards from rendezvousing with the Duke of Alma

Bess, thought to have been designed by Nicholas Hilliard, better known as a painter of miniatures. The Latin inscription round the edge signifies 'enclosing the most precious treasure in the world'—that is, the Queen herself. On the reverse (or 'tails' side) the safety of the kingdom is represented by a bay tree growing on a little island, immune from the flashes of lightning which seem to strike it. This medal, and a similar type showing the Ark floating calmly on a stormy sea, had loops at the top so that a chain or cord could be passed through it for suspension from the neck of the recipient. The so-called 'Ark in Flood' medal was produced during the reign of James I and was awarded to leading political figures and high-ranking officers. This medal, incidentally, exists in two versions, differing in the portrait of the king. The 'military' version showed him clad in armour, while the 'civil' version, given to his courtiers, depicted him in lace ruff and broad-brimmed hat.

The Civil War was the first campaign in which medals were awarded specifically for acts of bravery, rather than as a token of regard to leading generals. At his Court held at Oxford, in May 1643, King Charles I instituted medals 'to be delivered to wear on the breast of every man who shall be certified under the hands of their commanders-in-chief to have done us faithful service in the forlorn hope.' Two Forlorn Hope medals were produced, portraying the King and his son (later Charles II) respectively. These medals, issued generally for bravery, were preceded by a gold medal which the King awarded to Robert Welch for saving the royal standard at the Battle of Edgehill on 23 October 1642, the first battle of the war. This unique award depicted the standard on the reverse and bore a Latin inscription paying tribute to Welch.

The first campaign medal in the modern sense dates from the same period. In September 1650 the Roundheads under Oliver Cromwell defeated the Scots at Dunbar. The House of Commons voted that a medal should be struck and presented to all officers and men serving in the Parliamentary Army on that occasion. The Dunbar medal was engraved by Thomas Simon and issued in gold to officers and in silver to other ranks. The obverse portrayed Oliver Cromwell 'warts and all', while the reverse showed the interior of the House of Commons.

This precedent was never followed up, and almost 150 years elapsed before medals were again awarded generally to everyone who took

James I of England and VI of Scotland issued medals with his own portrait on them to notables of the time

facing page, Oliver Cromwell who became the Protector of England had a medal struck in his honour by order of Parliament after the Battle of Dunbar

General Sir George Elliott was the Governor and Commander of Gibraltar during the great siege

The obverse of Mr Boulton's Trafalgar medal struck in bronze-gilt. Much of the gilding has worn off
SPINK & SON

The reverse of the same medal
SPINK & SON

part in a battle or campaign. In the intervening years, however, medals were occasionally awarded for outstanding services as before. Naval medals were struck in gold for award to admirals and captains during the First Dutch War (1650–53), and the Battle of Culloden (1746) was marked by a medal portraying the 'Butcher' Cumberland and granted to officers who took part in the defeat of Bonnie Prince Charlie.

Towards the end of the eighteenth century the fashion for military awards increased slightly. During the American War of Independence, for example, a medal was awarded to a Captain Ewing for distinguished conduct at the Battle of Bunker Hill in 1776. No other medals or decorations were awarded on either side until 1782 when General George Washington instituted an award known as the Purple Heart. This was not a medal in the accepted sense, but consisted of a piece of purple cloth in the shape of a heart, trimmed with silver thread. This decoration came into existence too late, for the War of Independence was almost over, and it is thought that only three men received the award for conspicuous military service. The Purple Heart fell into disuse and it was not until 1932, as part of the celebrations marking the bicentenary of the birth of George Washington, that it was revived in a different form and for a different purpose which is described more fully in Chapter 4.

Much of the credit for instituting military medals must go to private individuals who used their own initiative and sense of public spirit to produce medals for award to officers and men in various campaigns, when the government overlooked the occasion. The successful defence of Gibraltar during the siege of 1779–83 was celebrated by several medals of an unofficial nature which were conferred on the defenders by General Elliott, the commander of Gibraltar.

Following the Battle of the Nile on 1 August 1798, Lord Nelson's Prize Agent, Alexander Davison, issued a medal at his own expense to every officer and seaman who took part in the engagement. The medal was struck in gold for award to admirals and captains, in silver for lieutenants and warrant officers, in gilt-bronze for petty officers and in bronze for seamen and marines. The cost of these medals to Mr. Davison was about £2,000. Seven years later he was not so generous. For the Battle of Trafalgar he struck a medal in pewter surrounded by a copper rim. The seamen of H.M.S. *Victory*, to whom it was awarded, were so disgusted at the base metal that

The Death of Nelson by Dieghton which also shows the general fighting activity on the *Victory* during the Battle of Trafalgar

they threw their medals into the sea! Matthew Boulton, of the Soho Mint in Birmingham, presented gold, silver and pewter medals to all the senior and junior officers and seamen who took part in the Battle of Trafalgar in October 1805. These medals, though privately issued, were given with official blessing and were worn by the recipients.

While the British government hesitated to make official awards for military service the Honourable East India Company was more enthusiastic. As early as 1668 the Company had instituted awards to officers for distinguished service in India and the Far East, but the first award of medals to all officers and men for services in a particular campaign occurred in 1784 when a medal was given to the Bengal Army for service in the West of India. A second medal was awarded the following year to a contingent from the Bengal Army which had served in the Carnatic campaign. Further awards were made regularly in subsequent campaigns, from the Mysore War of 1791 to the Burmese War of 1824–5. These medals were struck in bronze and were awarded to native soldiers only. An exception to this, however, was the medal awarded to all ranks who took part in the Battle of Seringapatam in 1799. Award of this medal was sanctioned by the Company in 1801. Generals and senior officers received the medal in gold, lieutenant-colonels, majors and staff officers in silver-gilt, captains and subalterns in silver, bronze for native commissioned and European non-commissioned officers, and pure tin to native and European privates. There was a curious delay in sending out the medals to India and it was not until 1809 that the recipients actually got them. The Seringapatam Medal showed the British lion attacking a tiger, emblem of Tippoo Sultan. The medal was often worn with a ribbon of blue-edged crimson (the Army colours) but sometimes a ribbon of pale orange was used, alluding to the fur of the tiger, Tippoo's favourite animal.

Official permission for officers of the Company's

Frederick I of Prussia founded the *Ordre Pour le Mérite* or the Blue Max as it later
was known. It was the highest Prussian, and afterwards German, award

left Lord Dalhousie was the first to suggest that a general medal should be awarded for service in India. *above* Franklin D Roosevelt instituted various gallantry awards during the second World War. *below* Emperor Hirohito of Japan awarded medals to his armies for their campaigns in Manchuria and China during the 1930s

The obverse and reverse of the Duke of Wellington's Seringa patam medal. It was awarded in 1799 by the Honourable East India Company

Army to wear this medal was not granted by the British government until 1815. Officers and men of the British Army present at the battle were not given permission to wear the medal until 1851— half a century after it was awarded!

The Napoleonic Wars

Government recognition, though slow in coming, first appeared during the long wars with France which began in 1792 and ended with the defeat of Napoleon at Waterloo in 1815. Admiral Lord Howe's defeat of the French fleet on 'the glorious first of June' 1794 was celebrated by the issue of a pair of gold medals, the larger one being given to admirals and the smaller one to ships' captains. The medals were suspended from white ribbons with blue edges. Admirals wore their medals from a ribbon round their necks while captains wore theirs from a button-hole on the left breast. The obverse showed an ancient galley with the winged figure of Nike, goddess of victory, on the prow placing a laurel wreath on the head of Britannia. The name of the recipient was engraved on the reverse. These medals are rare, the larger version having been awarded to Lord Howe and five subordinate flag officers and the smaller

Tippoo Sahib's Tiger was captured by the British after Seringapatam. It savages the soldier who struggles when the clockwork mechanism is wound up

version to fourteen captains.

Similar medals were later awarded to admirals and captains for the battles of St. Vincent (1797), Camperdown (1797), the Nile (1798) and Trafalgar (1805), as well as for a number of important single-ship actions. A notable exception was the Battle of Copenhagen (1801) which passed unnoticed. Much to Nelson's disgust, the government refused to award medals for this battle for fear of upsetting the Danes. Altogether 22 large and 117 small gold naval medals were awarded.

Over a decade elapsed before this idea was extended to the Army. In 1806 Major-General Sir John Stuart defeated the French at Maida in southern Italy. To mark this victory an Army gold medal was instituted and subsequently awarded to the thirteen senior officers who took part. The obverse bore a portrait of King George III while the reverse showed the goddess of Victory, Britannia and the three-legged symbol of the Kingdom of Naples and Sicily. The medal was suspended by a crimson ribbon with blue borders.

Four years later, following the successes of the Peninsular Campaign, it was decided to establish a pair of gold medals of uniform design, differing only in the name of the battle inscribed on the reverse. The first battles to be thus commemorated were Roleia, Vimiera, Sahagun, Benevente, Corunna and Talavera, which took place in 1808–9. Like the naval medals there was a larger version for award to generals and a smaller version for officers of field rank (majors and above). Both medals showed Britannia in a seated position, with the name of the battle engraved within a laurel wreath on the reverse. Subsequently army gold medals were issued for such battles as Barossa and Albuera in Spain, but also included the capture of Martinique and Guadeloupe in the West Indies (1809–10) and Java in the East Indies (1811), while several of the later awards marked battles in the War of 1812 against the United States—Chateauguay and Chrystler's Farm (both 1813) and the battles of Orthes and Toulouse (1814) which led to the defeat of Napoleon.

Unlike the naval medals, an officer could only receive one medal. Later awards took the form of a bar, suitably engraved with the name of the battle, which was attached to the ribbon. Where an officer was granted an award for four battles a large gold cross took the place of medal and bars, and in this instance the names of the battles were

Reverse of the gold Java Medal awarded in 1811 by the Honourable East India Company
SPINK & SON
beneath The Duke of Wellington's gold Peninsular Medal, obverse and reverse

A watercolour of part of the Battle of Talavera which took place in 1809 during the Peninsula campaigns

The Duke of Wellington's Peninsular Cross with nine bars mounted on a blue-edged crimson ribbon

engraved on the arms of the cross. Bars for further victories were then added to the ribbon of the cross. Of the large and small medals 469 were awarded without bars, 143 with one bar and 72 with two bars. There were 61 gold crosses without bars, 46 with one bar, 18 with two bars, 17 with three, 8 with four, 7 with five, 3 with six and 2 with seven bars. The cross awarded to the Duke of Wellington alone had nine bars which, with the names inscribed on the cross itself, represented distinguished service in thirteen battles. The system of adding bars to medals for second and subsequent awards was thus established. Incidentally collectors usually differentiate between *bars* marking subsequent awards for gallantry and *clasps* indicating subsequent awards to campaign medals for later battles and campaigns. The two terms are often used indiscriminately. The blue-edged crimson ribbon used with these medals and crosses was later used for the Waterloo Medal of 1815, the Army General Service Medal authorized in 1848, and remains in use to this day as the ribbon of the Distinguished Service Order, instituted in 1886.

The Battle of the Nile painted by Pocock

above, An engraving of the storming of Kewmendine near Rangoon during the first Burma war

2 BRITISH CAMPAIGN MEDALS

Although the Army gold medal is known to have been awarded to eleven officers of the British and Spanish armies below the rank of major, and even to a warrant officer—Sergeant-Major Don Santiago Ruiz—junior officers, warrant officers, N.C.O.s and enlisted men were not eligible as a rule for this decoration. The rank and file might have gone unremembered had it not been for the dramatic events of Napoleon's Hundred Days— his escape from Elba, his return to France, and the short campaign which ended with the Battle of Waterloo on 18 June 1815. This decisive victory, which brought Napoleon's ambitions to an end, was celebrated by the award of a silver medal to all ranks of the British Army, the first such award since 1650 and the first campaign medal in the modern sense.

The Waterloo Medal bore the portrait of the Prince Regent (later King George IV) on the obverse and featured the goddess of victory and the date of the battle on the reverse. Originally the medal was issued with a large steel ring for suspension— a curious note of economy which did not appeal to most of the recipients who substituted silver

The Duke of Wellington's Waterloo medal with original steel clip ring, obverse and reverse. It has a blue-edged crimson ribbon

George IV took a great interest in the struggle against Napoleon while he was Prince Regent. He personally designed the Field Marshal's Baton that he sent to the Duke of Wellington

rings or bars. Examples of the medal with the original steel ring are therefore comparatively scarce. The medal was awarded to all troops who took part in the Battle of Waterloo itself, as well as those who had fought in the Battles of Ligny and Quatre Bras two days earlier. The reverse of the medal also bore the name of the commander-in-chief, the Duke of Wellington—an honour which has been bestowed on no general since that time.

The name of the recipient was inscribed on the rim of the medal, a practice which has continued with most British campaign medals down to the present day. This fact enhances the value and interest of medals to the collector. Each medal was once awarded to a soldier, seaman or airman because he was present at some historic battle or took part in a campaign. Not only his name is given, but his regimental or unit number, his regiment, ship or military formation. The collector can therefore identify the recipient of a medal and with luck and a certain amount of research can trace the career of the person to whom the medal was awarded.

The name inscribed on a medal can affect its value considerably. With the Waterloo Medal, for example, those awarded to men in General Colville's Division (2/35, 1/54, 2/59 and 1/91 Foot regiments) are not so highly regarded, and therefore not so valuable, on account of the fact that this Division was out on the right flank during the battle and took no part in the actual fighting.

Naval and Military General Service Medals

The fact that senior officers of the Navy and Army had received medals and crosses for the Napoleonic campaigns but not the junior officers and other ranks created a great deal of ill feeling and from time to time it was suggested that medals should be struck and awarded to veterans of the Napoleonic Wars. Nevertheless nothing was done about this until 1847—32 years after the war had ended. The award of Naval and Military General Service Medals was sanctioned by Queen Victoria whose profile appeared on the obverse of both medals with the date 1848. The reverse of the naval medal showed Britannia seated on a sea-horse while the reverse of the military medal showed Queen Victoria placing a wreath of laurel on the head of the Duke of Wellington. The naval medal had no inscription on the reverse but the military medal was inscribed TO THE BRITISH ARMY and bore the dates 1793–1814 in the exergue (the space at the foot of the design).

Since applications for these medals were in some cases made in respect of campaigns more than fifty years earlier, it is hardly surprising that the number of medals awarded was comparatively small, while the number of bars awarded for certain battles and engagements was quite minute. Some 25,650 applications were received in respect of the Military General Service Medal and 20,901 for its naval counterpart. No fewer than 29 different bars were authorised for the military medal, but a total of 231 different bars was authorised for the naval medal—proof of the power and ubiquity of the Royal Navy 150 years ago. Paradoxically multiples of bars are commoner for the military medal than the naval medal. Two soldiers received the former with fifteen bars and more than a dozen were awarded fourteen bars, whereas the record for the latter medal is seven bars (two recipients) while five men received six bars and fourteen got five. The number of possible combinations of bars with the Naval General Service Medal is infinitely greater.

The Military General Service Medal was restricted to land campaigns during the Peninsular War (1808–13), the American War (1812–14) and isolated actions in the West Indies, Egypt and Java, whereas the Naval General Service Medal covered a far longer period, ranging from the capture of the French frigate *La Cleopatra* by H.M.S. *Nymphe* in June 1793, to the naval blockade of the Syrian coast in 1840 during the British operations against Mehemet Ali. Other naval campaigns after the Napoleonic period for which bars were awarded were Algiers (August 1815) and the Battle of Navarino (October 1827). Naval medals with the bar for Syria are relatively plentiful (7,057 were awarded), but at the other end of the scale there were several instances in which bars were awarded to a single applicant and in seven cases there were no claimants for bars at all. It should be remembered that applications for the medals and bars resulted mainly from the publicity given by printed advertisements and notices posted up all over the country. With the poor general standard of literacy at the time, many people who were entitled to the medals would have been quite unaware of their existence. Moreover, many people who would have been entitled to the medals and bars had died long before the awards were authorised.

The scarcer bars awarded to the Naval General Service Medal were those for 'Boat Service'. Altogether there were 55 bars of this type which

The Military General Service Medal was issued in 1848. It was mounted on a blue-edged crimson ribbon. The reverse is shown *SPINK & SON*

The reverse of the Naval General Service Medal 1793-1814 which was issued in 1848. It covered the period from 1793 to 1840 and had a white ribbon with blue edges *SPINK & SON*

The 1st Berkshire Regiment in action at the Battle of Tofrek in the Sudan in 1885

were sanctioned for minor engagements involving ships' boats in which one or more officers were promoted as a result. The largest scale boat action was that which took place off New Orleans on 14 December 1814, involving the destruction of the American guard-ships; this resulted in the award of 214 bars. The next most plentiful bars are those for Boat Service dated 1 November 1809 (118), 23 November 1810 (65) and April and May 1813 (55), while in five cases only one bar is known to have been awarded. Medals with any of these rare bars are highly prized and fetch huge sums whenever they appear at auction.

Other General Service Medals

Apart from several medals which were mainly awarded to troops of the Honourable East India Company, and are dealt with later in this chapter, the earliest medals to appear after the Naval and Military General Service Medals of 1848 were likewise general in character. Although many individual campaigns and wars of the nineteenth and twentieth centuries have resulted in distinctive medals, it was found convenient and economic to group many of the minor campaigns together and issue a general service medal with appropriate bars.

The first of these appeared in 1851 and is known as the First India Medal. It was awarded to troops who had served in various Indian campaigns from 1799 to 1826. These dates appear on the reverse, below a seated goddess of Victory, with the inscription THE ARMY OF INDIA. Altogether 21 bars were awarded with this medal, ranging from Allighur (1803) to Bhurtpoor (1826). This medal was designed as the counterpart of the Military General Service Medal, for award to troops who had served in India. The medal was authorised in 1851 and was provided at the expense of the Honourable East India Company.

Three years later there appeared the India General Service Medal, first awarded to personnel who served in the Burmese War of 1852–3. The medal was introduced on the recommendation of Lord Dalhousie, Governor-General of India, who suggested that a general service medal should be issued for award to troops taking part in minor campaigns. In the years between 1839 and 1850 eight different medals had been issued for wars and campaigns in India and it was felt that a general medal would be less expensive.

The India GSM remained in use until 1895 and in that period was awarded for service in 23 different wars and expeditions ranging from Persia

The reverse of the Army of India Medal, 1799-1826. This was the first of the 'regular' medals issued by the Honourable East India Company in 1851. It was mounted on a pale blue ribbon *SPINK & SON*

The reverse of the India General Service Medal which was issued to cover the period 1854-1895. It has a red ribbon with two dark blue stripes

The reverse of the second India General Service Medal which was issued between 1895 and 1902. It has a purple ribbon with two green stripes
SPINK & SON

The reverse of the third India General Service Medal which was issued between 1908 and 1935. It has a green ribbon with a broad blue stripe down the centre
SPINK & SON

left to right The reverse of the South Africa Medal 1877-9. The reverse of the East & West Africa Medal 1887-1906 which was mounted on a yellow and black striped ribbon. The Central Africa Medal had the identical obverse and reverse, but a ribbon with three equal stripes of black, brown and white. The reverse of the Africa General Service Medal which was first issued in 1902. It has a black and yellow striped ribbon
SPINK & SON

and the North-west Frontier to Perak in Malaysia. By the time of the Chitral campaign in 1895 it was felt that a new medal should be issued. The India Medal which appeared the following year may be found with seven different bars and the profile of Queen Victoria. A new version of the medal, with the portrait of King Edward VII on the obverse and the date 1895 removed from the reverse, appeared in 1903. Only one bar, for Waziristan, was issued with the King's medal. Soldiers who already had the Queen's medal were merely given a bar for Waziristan added to their existing medal.

A new India GSM was introduced in December 1908 and remained in use till 1935. It may be found with the portraits of King Edward VII or King George V on the obverse. An interesting bar is that for Waziristan 1925 which was only awarded to Royal Air Force personnel. The last issue of the India General Service Medal was authorised in 1936 and bore the effigy of King George VI on the obverse and a tiger on the reverse. This medal had two bars only, for service on the North-west Frontier in 1936–37 and 1937–39.

Many of the minor colonial wars and expeditions of the nineteenth century took place in Africa and several general service medals were struck for that purpose. The first of these, inscribed SOUTH AFRICA was issued in 1854 for service in the Kaffir Wars of 1834–35, 1846–47 and 1850–53. The same medal with a trophy of weapons instead of the date was subsequently issued with bars bearing dates from 1879 to 1887 in various combinations for service in campaigns against different tribes. The medal, without distinguishing bar, was awarded for service in the Zulu War.

A medal was awarded to soldiers who took part in the expedition of 1873–74 against the King of Ashantee in the Gold Coast (now Ghana). This medal was revived in 1887 and is known as the East and West Africa Medal. Soldiers and sailors who served in various minor African expeditions between 1887 and 1900 received this medal with the appropriate bar. Subsequently there were distinctive medals for service in various campaigns in East and Central Africa (1891–98 and 1897–99) and a comparatively rare Cape of Good Hope General Service Medal in 1900 to cover native wars from 1880 onwards. The last of the Africa General Service Medals appeared in 1902 and bore the profile of King Edward VII on the obverse and the figure of Britannia with the British lion on the reverse. Numerous bars were issued for service in various parts of Africa up to the time of King

Edward's death in 1910. The medal was revived six years later, with the effigy of King George V, and bars were awarded for participation in minor campaigns against African tribes, from the Shimber Berris expedition against the dervishes of Somaliland in 1914 to the Somali campaign against the Mad Mullah in 1920. The same ribbon and the same reverse design were used for a new Africa General Service Medal instituted in 1955, with a portrait of Queen Elizabeth on the obverse. This medal, with bar inscribed KENYA, was awarded to troops who took part in the operations against the Mau Mau terrorists. No other bars have so far been awarded with this medal.

A Naval General Service Medal was introduced in 1915 and was first awarded retrospectively to officers and men who served in the Persian Gulf area from 1909 to 1914. Subsequent bars were awarded for service on the coasts of Iraq and Persia in 1919–20. The medal was revived in May 1940, with the effigy of King George VI in place of King George V. The first bar of this medal was awarded for naval service off the coast of Palestine in 1938–39. Subsequent bars marked service in South-East Asia in 1945–46, minesweeping operations and bomb disposal after the Second World War, and naval patrol service in Palestine or Malayan waters. An interesting bar is that inscribed YANGTSE 1949, which was awarded to the crews of naval gunboats patrolling this river at the time when the Chinese Communists came to power. Medals awarded to the crew of HMS *Amethyst* are particularly prized by collectors, on account of the daring exploits of its captain, Lieutenant Commander Kerans, subsequently filmed as *The Yangtse Incident*. This medal, with the portrait of Queen Elizabeth, is still in use, though only one bar, for bomb/mine clearance, has so far been awarded.

A General Service Medal, for the Army and the Royal Air Force, was instituted in 1918 for award with distinctive bars in connection with minor campaigns which did not justify the award of separate medals. Three versions of this medal were issued, differing in the portrait of the monarch (King George V, King George VI and Queen Elizabeth) and bars have ranged from Iraq and Kurdistan (1918) to the more recent conflicts in Suez, Cyprus, Malaya and Aden. A new military general service medal was instituted in 1962 and first awarded for service in Borneo. The ribbon of the previous medal was purple with a green band in the centre. The new medal has a green ribbon with purple borders. The most recent bar

A watercolour of tribesmen firing from a hillside on the North West Frontier of India. This border was never completely quiet throughout the whole period of British rule

The obverse of the General Service Medal which was first issued in 1918 and is awarded to both Army and R.A.F. It has a dark blue ribbon with a central green stripe

A typical scene after the engagements in the Crimea as shown
by Lady Butler in her painting *Roll Call*

right The obverse and reverse of the Burma Medal which was awarded
for services in the First Burma War, 1824-6 by the Hon. East India
Company. It should have an edged ribbon
The obverse of the Ghuznee Medal of 1839. It has a halved ribbon of
red and green
The obverse and reverse of the Meeanee-Hyderabad Scinde Campaign
Medal, issued in 1843. It has a white watered silk ribbon with edges of
red and blue and a gold centre
The obverse of the Maharajpoor Star of the Gwalior Campaign of 1843. It
still has its original hook on the reverse for putting through a button
hole or pocket
The reverse of the Sutlej Campaign Medal of 1845-6. It has a red-edged
blue ribbon
The reverse of the Punjab Campaign Medal of 1848-9. It has a dark blue
ribbon with two narrow yellow stripes very close to the edges
SPINK & SON

awarded to this medal is for service in Ireland since 1969. Oddly enough military service in Ireland during the Easter Rising of 1916 and the 'Troubles' of 1919–21 went unmarked by the award of medals, no doubt because of the politically sensitive nature of what was virtually a civil war.

Specific Campaign Medals

Apart from the various general service medals distinctive awards have been made for certain wars and campaigns. At first these medals were awarded by the Honourable East India Company to the Madras and Bengal native troops employed in the Company's wars and expeditions, in much the same way as the medals of the late eighteenth century had been awarded. Medals commemorated service in the First Burma War (1824–26); the capture of Ghuznee (1839); the campaigns of 1842 around Jellalabad, Ghuznee, Cabul and Kelat-i-Ghilzie; the Sinde Medal (1843); the stars for the Gwalior campaign (1843) and the medals for the Sutlej campaign (1845–46) and the Punjab (1848–49). As has been noted above, the India General Service Medal of 1854 did away with the need for separate medals for subsequent campaigns, though there were several notable exceptions.

The first medal granted to British forces since Waterloo was authorised in 1842 for soldiers and sailors who had taken part in the campaigns against China in 1841–42 resulting in the capture of Hong Kong. The war with Russia in 1854–56 resulted in two medals, one for service on board ships in the Baltic Sea and the other for service in the Crimea. No bars were issued with the Baltic medal, but bars inscribed with the names of Inkerman, Alma, Balaklava, Sebastopol and Azoff were awarded to the Crimea Medal. Medals with the bar 'Balaklava' and bearing the names of personnel of the 17th Lancers, 13th Light Dragoons, 11th Hussars, 4th Light Dragoons and the 8th Hussars are most highly prized by collectors since these were the regiments which took part in the historic Charge of the Light Brigade. The bars of the Crimea Medal are much more ornamental than those found on any other British medal, being in the form of oak leaves with the name inscribed across them.

A medal with a red and white ribbon was awarded to British troops engaged in quelling the Indian Mutiny of 1857–58. This was the last medal issued by the Honourable East India Company on behalf of the British government. Control of India

The reverse of the Baltic Medal for service between 1854 and 1855. It has an orange ribbon edged in pale blue
SPINK & SON

The reverse of the Crimean Medal, 1854-6. The bars are by far the most ornate of any medal. It has a yellow-edged pale blue ribbon
SPINK & SON

The reverse of the Indian Mutiny Medal of 1857-8. It has a white ribbon with two stripes of red
SPINK & SON

was transferred from the Company to the British government following the mutiny. Of the bars awarded to this medal that inscribed 'Defence of Lucknow' is most eagerly sought after. A new China Medal, similar to that of 1842, but with the date altered, was released in 1861 and awarded to soldiers and sailors who took part in operations in China between 1857 and 1860. Originally a new reverse design, showing the British lion trampling on the Chinese dragon, was produced, but it was scrapped for fear of giving offence to the late enemy, and the original design featuring a trophy of weapons was used instead.

Though no medal, prior to 1971, had commemorated military service in Ireland, it is interesting to note that Irish terrorist activity in another part of the world resulted in the award of a distinctive medal. The Fenians, ancestors of the Irish Republican Army of the present day, began rebellions in Canada in 1866 and 1870. For this purpose the Canada General Service Medal was authorised and bars inscribed 'Fenian Raid' and the respective dates were awarded. A third bar, inscribed 'Red River 1870' was awarded to troops who fought against the rebellion of Louis Riel. This medal, presented by the Canadian authorities, was not sanctioned until 1899.

The most unusual medal issued to British troops was the Abyssinian Medal awarded for service with the Napier Expedition of 1867–68. The circular part was smaller than usual and was surmounted by a crown through which the ring for the suspension of the ribbon was passed. It was the only medal in which the name of the recipient was embossed in the circular space on the reverse side.

The Afghan War of 1878–80 resulted in a medal for which six bars were awarded. The reverse featured an elephant carrying a mountain gun and the ribbon was supposed to represent crimson for Britain and green for the Prophet Mohammed. In addition troops who served under Lord Roberts in the epic march from Kabul to Kandahar in August 1880 were awarded a five-pointed star surmounted by a crown and bearing the royal monogram in the centre. This star was made from bronze taken from the guns captured at the Battle of Kandahar. The ribbon used with this star was identical to that used with the Jellalabad and Indian medals of 1842–43, of white watered silk with edges of red and blue and a gold centre.

The campaigns in Egypt and the Sudan in the 1880s resulted in a distinctive medal with a ribbon of blue and white stripes, said to represent the Blue and White Nile. At first this medal was awarded to the troops who took part in the expedition of 1882 against Arabi Pasha and depicted the Sphinx with the date 1882 beneath. The campaign dragged on for a further seven years and subsequent issues of the medal had the date deleted. Thirteen different engagement bars were awarded with this medal, ranging from the landing at Alexandria (July 1882) to the fighting at Toski (August 1889). Personnel who served in the campaign but did not actually take part in any of these battles were given the medal without any bars. A five-pointed bronze star was also awarded, by the Khedive of Egypt, to all British troops who received the Egypt Medal.

Troops who served on the expedition of 1895–96 to suppress human sacrifice in Ashanti territory were awarded the Ashanti Star, a four-

pointed star with a rectangular cross between the points. Queen Victoria's daughter, Princess Henry of Battenberg, designed this unusual award, in memory of her husband who died in this campaign.

The reconquest of the Sudan by General Kitchener in 1896–97 was marked by a medal authorised in 1899. No engagement bars were awarded, but it should be noted that the Khedive of Egypt again struck a medal for British troops and on this occasion several bars were awarded. The Khedive's Sudan Medal also covered the period up to 1908 and further bars were awarded for subsequent actions.

Towards the end of the nineteenth century medals were awarded by chartered companies for services rendered by British and colonial troops in the same way that the Honourable East India Company had awarded medals. The British South Africa Company awarded medals with similar designs for the campaigns in Mashonaland (1893), Rhodesia (1896) and Mashonaland (1897). In 1926 a bar inscribed 'Mashonaland 1890' was issued to those who had taken part in the pioneer expedition which led to the establishment of Rhodesia. The Royal Niger Company issued a medal in 1899 to troops who had served in its territory between 1886 and 1897, while the British North Borneo Company likewise issued medals in recognition of service between 1897 and 1916. Four different medals were issued, but officers and men who had already received an award merely got a bar for subsequent awards.

The Anglo-Boer War of 1899–1902 resulted in two medals usually known as the Queen's South African Medal and King Edward's South African Medal, from the portraits featured on the obverse.

The reverse of the second China War Medal of 1857-60. It has a yellow-edged purple ribbon. The obverse of the Abyssinian War Medal of 1867-8, which has a white-edged red ribbon. It is a very unusual design
The reverse of the Afghanistan Medal of 1878-80, which has a green-edged red ribbon
The reverse of the second issue of the Egypt Medal which was awarded from 1882 to 1889. The first issue was dated 1882 under the Sphinx. The ribbon was blue and white stripes
The obverse of the Khedive's Egypt Star; this is one of the issue dated 1882. It has a dark blue ribbon
SPINK & SON

The reverse of the Queen's Sudan Medal, authorised in 1899 for the campaign of 1896-7. It has a halved yellow and black ribbon with a narrow red stripe down the centre
The obverse of the Queen's South Africa Medal which was awarded from 1899 to 1902. The ribbon is red, blue and orange
The obverse of the King's South Africa Medal which was awarded in 1901 and 1902. It has a green, cream and orange ribbon.

A watercolour by R. Simmion of the charge of the Gordon Highlanders at Grobler's Kloof in 1899 during the Boer War

The reverse designs, showing Britannia advancing towards a party of soldiers, were identical and bore the inscription at the top. A similar design, inscribed MEDITERRANEAN at the top, was used for a medal awarded to militiamen who served in the Mediterranean garrisons during the Boer War, thereby releasing regular troops for active service in South Africa. Numerous bars were awarded with the Queen's medal, but only two were issued with the King's medal and were inscribed 'South Africa 1901' or 'South Africa 1902'. These medals tend to go in pairs, for no one received the King's medal unless he had already received the Queen's medal. On the other hand certain personnel who were eligible for the Queen's medal did not qualify for the King's medal but merely received the bars for 1901 or 1902 which were then worn on the Queen's medal. Both the Mayor of Kimberley and the Cape Copper Company awarded distinctive medals to troops engaged in the defence of Kimberley during the siege of 1899–1900 and the defence of Ookiep Mine in South West Africa, but as these medals were not officially authorised officers and men were not permitted to wear them.

The 1st Sikh Regiment scaling the walls of Peking during the Boxer Rebellion of 1900

The Boxer Rebellion in China in 1900 was put down by an international expedition. British troops were subsequently awarded a China Medal which was similar in design to the medal of 1842 but with the date altered. The crew of HMS *Terrible* had the unique distinction of receiving both the South African and the China Medals since their ship was the only one to take part in both campaigns that year.

Campaign medals portraying King Edward VII were awarded for the Ashanti rebellion of 1901, the Younghusband Expedition to Tibet in 1903–4 and the Zulu Rising of 1906. A Transport Medal was instituted in 1903 and awarded to Merchant Navy officers who served on board troopships involved in the South African and Chinese campaigns. It was originally intended that this medal should be given to Merchant Navy officers in subsequent wars and campaigns, but a separate medal was awarded in the First World War whereas officers and men of the Merchant Navy received the ordinary military stars and medals awarded to the Royal Navy in the Second World War.

In terms of its length and the number of troops engaged, the First World War deserved its

The reverse of the Tibet Medal which was awarded in 1904 to members of the Younghusband Expedition. The ribbon is purple with two white stripes and green edges. *right* The reverse of the Natal Rebellion Medal which was awarded after the Zulu Rising of 1906. It has a black-edged purple ribbon

The obverse of the 1914-15 Star which was awarded to anyone who did not receive the 1914 Star. It has a red, white and blue ribbon, the colours merging into each other

original name of the Great War. Nevertheless, in terms of medals authorised it was honoured less than the Boer War and many minor conflicts. The first award to appear was the 1914 Star, often, though incorrectly, called the Mons Star. This bronze star, embellished with crossed swords, was inscribed AUG–NOV 1914 and was awarded to personnel of the British and Indian Expeditionary Forces who served in France and Belgium in the opening campaign of the war. A bar inscribed with the actual dates of the campaign (5 August–22 November 1914) was authorised in 1919 and given to those troops who had actually served under fire in that campaign. The bar had four tiny holes, two at either end, so that it could be sewn on to the ribbon, rather than be fixed on to the suspender of the medal itself as was customary

with all previous medals. This rather clumsy, though economic, device was also used for the bars awarded to campaign stars in the Second World War.

The 1914–15 Star, sanctioned in 1918, was similar in design to the 1914 Star, with the dates in the centre altered and the scrolls inscribed 'Aug' and 'Nov' removed. This star was awarded to all personnel serving in any theatre of operations up to the end of 1915 who had not already received the 1914 Star. A special Gallipoli Star, to be given to troops of the Australia and New Zealand Army Corps (the 'Anzacs') was designed but never awarded as it was felt that such an award would have been unfair to those British troops who also served at Gallipoli. In the end the Anzacs had to be content with the 1914–15 Star.

Men from the 58th London Division Front going up to the front line in France, April 1918

The obverse of the British War Medal which was awarded for services between 1914 and 1920. It has a blue-edged orange ribbon with narrow black and white stripes. *right* The reverse of the Mercantile Marine War Medal which was awarded to sailors in the Merchant Navy. It has a halved orange and green ribbon with a white centre stripe

The British War Medal, struck in silver, was sanctioned in 1919 for award to all personnel who had been on active service for at least 28 days between 5 August 1914 and 11 November 1918. The date was later extended to 1920 to include troops who served in the Caspian and Baltic areas during the expeditions against the Bolsheviks in Russia. Initially it was intended to award engagement bars or clasps with this medal but though lists of bars were drawn up and authorised the idea was eventually scrapped on the grounds of cost. A total of 44 bars was authorised for naval personnel ranging from 'Heligoland, August 1914' to 'Caspian August 1919'. The proposals by the Army and the Royal Air Force were never published, but it seems probable that in those cases the number of bars would have been even greater.

A Mercantile Marine War Medal, struck in bronze, was issued to officers and men of the Merchant Navy who had made at least one voyage in a war zone. In many cases these men were also eligible for the British War Medal and the Victory

Medal. The Victory Medal, made in a brass alloy, featured the goddess of victory on the obverse and the inscription THE GREAT WAR FOR CIVILIZATION on the reverse. The medal was of a design uniform to all the Allies and the same ribbon, of watered silk in the colours of the rainbow, was used by all the countries concerned —the first instance of international co-operation in the award of medals. Another innovation with this medal was the oak leaf which was worn on the ribbon to denote that the recipient had been mentioned in despatches. A smaller version of this oak leaf was worn on the piece of ribbon sewn on uniform when the full medal was not worn. Only one oak leaf was worn, no matter how many times the holder of the medal had been mentioned in despatches. The last of the military awards for the First World War was the bronze Territorial Force War Medal, awarded to members of the Territorial Force (later known as the Territorial Army) who had volunteered for active service on or before 30 September 1914.

The obverse of the Victory Medal which has a design and ribbon uniform to all the Allies. The ribbon is rainbow coloured. *right* The reverse of the Territorial War Medal which was awarded to Territorial Force Members who volunteered before 1st October 1914. The ribbon is yellow with two narrow blue stripes

Members of the 2nd Battalion, North Staffordshire Regiment and the Royal Tank Regiment on an exercise at Hebuterne in northern France in 1940

Royal Marine Commando troops landing during
the invasion of Europe in 1944

left to right The obverse of the Pacific Star which has a red-edged green ribbon with a central yellow stripe and other stripes of dark and light blue. The obverse of the Burma Star which has a dark blue, red and orange ribbon. The obverse of the Italy Star which has a green, white and red ribbon. The obverse of the France and Germany Star which has a red, white and blue ribbon

There were no campaign medals awarded in the period between the two World Wars, the various general service medals covering all the minor campaigns of that time. The Second World War, however, was far better served for medals than the First World War, there being eight bronze campaign stars and two cupro-nickel medals. The six-pointed campaign stars were uniform in design, with the crown and royal cypher in the middle and the name of the campaign inscribed in a circle. The 1939–45 Star (dark blue, red and light blue ribbon) was given for six months operational service outside the United Kingdom between 3 September 1939 and 15 August 1945. The Atlantic Star (blue, white and green ribbon of watered silk) was awarded primarily to naval personnel who served in the Battle of the Atlantic. The Air Crew Europe Star (pale blue with black edges and narrow yellow stripes) was awarded to air crew for operational flights from 3 September 1939 till 4 June 1944. The Africa Star (buff ribbon with dark blue, red and light blue stripes) was awarded to personnel who served in North Africa and Italian East Africa between 10 June 1940 and 12 May 1943. Silver numerals '1' or '8' worn on the ribbon indicated service with the First or Eighth Armies. The Pacific Star (dark green ribbon with red edges, central yellow stripe and stripes of dark and light blue) was given for active service in the Pacific theatre of operations between 8 December 1941 and 15 August 1945, when Japan surrendered. The Burma Star (dark blue, red and orange ribbon) was awarded to troops who served in the Burma campaign from 11 December 1941 onwards. The Italy Star (green, white and red ribbon) was awarded for active service in Italy and the eastern Mediterranean from 11 June 1943 after Italy went over to the Allies, to 8 May 1945. The France and Germany Star (red, white and blue ribbon) was given for active service in western Europe after the D-Day invasion of Normandy on 6 June 1944, to the unconditional surrender of Germany on 8 May 1945.

A Hurricane squadron on patrol during the Battle of Britain

facing page Members of the 8th Army advancing in the desert

For reasons of economy certain stars were replaced by engagement bars worn on the ribbons of previous stars awarded. Thus it was impossible to wear both the Atlantic Star and the Air Crew Europe or France and Germany Stars. The latter awards were given in the form of bars. Conversely if the Air Crew Europe or France and Germany Stars were first awarded, second and third awards would be recognised by the appropriate bar. Personnel qualifying for both Pacific and Burma stars wore only the first of these stars, and a bar denoting the second award. The Italy Star was awarded in addition to any other star and had no bars of its own. A bar inscribed 'North Africa 1942–43' was given to holders of the Africa Star for service in certain areas between 23 October 1942 and 12 May 1943 where they were not eligible for the First or Eighth Army bars. The rarest, and most coveted, of the Second World War bars was that inscribed 'Battle of Britain', awarded to air crews of fighter aircraft engaged in the Battle of Britain between 1 July and 31 October 1940. When the ribbons alone are worn these bars are represented by small silver rosettes, a gilt rosette representing the Battle of Britain bar.

The obverse and reverse of the Defence Medal which has a green-edged flame-coloured ribbon with narrow black stripes. *below* The reverse of the War Medal which has a broad red and blue and narrow red and white striped ribbon

In addition to the campaign stars there were two medals. The Defence Medal (flame-coloured ribbon with green edges and narrow black stripes) was awarded to civilian personnel or military forces not on active service for service in the United Kingdom itself over a period of three years. This explains why many servicemen, awarded various campaign stars, did not qualify for the Defence Medal. The War Medal (red, white and blue ribbon) was awarded to all full-time personnel of the armed forces (excluding the Home Guard) wherever they served during the war, the minimum period being 28 days between 3 September 1939 and 2 September 1945. This medal was granted in addition to the campaign stars, so that anyone who had been awarded a campaign star automatically qualified for the War Medal. Both the Defence and War Medals were struck in cupro-nickel, though examples in silver, awarded to Canadian forces, may be encountered. In addition, Canada, Australia, India, New Zealand, South Africa and Southern Rhodesia issued their own distinctive war medals for service during the war. In certain instances British personnel were eligible for these awards.

The reverse of the Korean War Medal which has a yellow and blue ribbon in five equal stripes

Since the Second World War Britain has produced only one distinctive campaign medal, to mark the Korean War of 1950–53. The ribbon is yellow and blue, in five equal stripes, and the reverse shows Hercules fighting the Hydra, a mythical monster with nine heads. Recipients of this medal, incidentally, automatically qualified for the award of the United Nations medal with the clasp for Korea. This medal, featuring the UN emblem, was struck in a bronze alloy and is worn with a ribbon of blue and white stripes, the United Nations colours. The British Korea Medal was normally struck in cupro-nickel, but Canadian forces were awarded the medal in silver. This version also has the word CANADA below the Queen's head on the obverse.

Men of the 41st Commandos (Royal Marines) in combat dress during the Korean War

The Naming of British Medals

The Military and Naval General Service Medals, with their multitudinous combinations of bars, have long been popular with collectors, but the other campaign medals of the past 120 years have a strong following as well. With the exception of the stars and medals of the Second World War, all British campaign medals have borne the name of the recipient and usually his or her number, regiment, unit and rank as well. This brings a personal element into the study of medals which is lacking in most other collecting hobbies. The name on a medal is very important for two reasons. It is a means of testing the genuineness, not only of the medal itself, but its bar combination, and secondly it enables the collector to link the medal not only with the man who won it, but with his unit or formation, and thus plays a vital part in the development of naval or military history, if only a small part in most cases.

Much of the value of a medal to the collector depends on the man who won it, or the unit to which he belonged. Since it would be impossible to collect medals in a general fashion, the collector must specialise in some aspect of the subject, restricting his interests perhaps to one medal (for example, British campaigns in India) or to medals and decorations awarded to the men of one regiment. The information given on the rim or back of a medal is therefore important in helping to identify it and assign it to its correct place. Even this has to be qualified to some extent. Some regiments are more popular than others with collectors and much depends on the part, active or passive, played by a unit in a particular battle or campaign for which the medal was awarded. Then again, the combination of event with the particular regiment of the recipient has to be considered.

At one extreme we find that the Royal Regiment of Artillery, living up to its motto *'Ubique'* (everywhere), can claim to have won almost every campaign medal available. Among the few instances of soldiers being awarded the Atlantic Star, for example, are Maritime Gunners—soldiers who manned the anti-aircraft guns on certain ships during the Battle of the Atlantic. At the other extreme one finds odd detachments, sometimes consisting of one or two men only, seconded from a regiment for service with another unit.

The Indian General Service Medal, with bar for Hazara 1891, is usually found named to personnel of the 11th Bengal Lancers and various battalions of the Bengal Infantry, but according to the medal rolls it was also given to six men of the 2nd Manchester Regiment, two men of the Queen's Regiment and one each to troopers of the 2nd and 7th Dragoon Guards. Whereas a specimen of this medal with this bar is not hard to find named to a soldier of one of the Bengal units it is a major rarity when awarded to one of the 'odd men' and its value is correspondingly high.

Since the personal details given on a medal regarding the recipient are so important, it is necessary for the collector to verify two facts—that the person whose name is on the medal was actually present at the action for which either the medal or its bars were awarded, and secondly, that the naming of the bar and the attachment of the bars is correct and not tampered with in any way. As regards the first, the Public Record Office in Chancery Lane, London, is a goldmine of information for all naval and military campaigns. Apart from despatches, reports and muster rolls covering the actions, there are the medal rolls compiled from applications for medals and bars. Transcriptions of the medal rolls are held by regimental museums in many cases, and also by such bodies as the Military Historical Association.

These rolls, while extremely useful, have to be used with caution. The presence of a name on the roll does not mean that a medal or bar was inevitably awarded; conversely authenticated medals are known to exist named to persons not listed on the medal roll. There are often discrepancies between the muster and medal rolls. Moreover discrepancies in the spelling of recipients' names are not uncommon and bars are sometimes found listed for regiments which were not even in existence at the time when a battle was fought! This is explained, however, by the fact that a man may have been serving with one unit which took part in the campaign and subsequently transferred to another. When claiming the medal he probably gave his *present* unit, rather than the one in which he was serving at the time of the action.

Unfortunately cases of medals having been tampered with are by no means rare, so it is necessary to be able to recognise evidence of fakery. A favourite device of the faker is to alter the name and personal details of the recipient and to substitute another name in order to enhance the medal's value. This is done simply by filing the inscription off the rim and adding a new one. In order to check a medal for such alterations a similar medal of proven genuineness should be compared with the suspect and their diameters checked carefully with a pair of fine callipers. Take the measurements at several points round the rim so that any unevenness should soon be apparent.

I cannot stress too much the importance of being closely familiar with the various styles of naming medals. This problem is dealt with in great detail by Alec A. Purves in his book *Collecting Medals and Decorations* (published by B. A. Seaby, 1968).

An incredible variety of lettering—roman, italic, script, sans-serif, seriffed in all shapes and sizes—has been used at one time or another. In some cases the lettering has been applied by impressing; in others the inscription is engraved by hand. If a medal is normally impressed and you come across an engraved example you should immediately be on your guard. This is not an infallible test, however, since medals have been known with more than one style of lettering, particularly if duplicates were issued at a much later date to replace medals lost or destroyed.

A cunning approach was adopted by some fakers in respect of the Naval General Service Medal. The three commonest bars Algiers (1,362), Navarino (1,137) and Syria (7,057) were awarded to many recipients possessing common names such as Jones or Smith which can be matched with recipients of some very rare bars. In the case of the NGSM the ship on which the recipient served is not given, thus aiding the fraudulent substitution of bars. It is necessary, therefore, to check the condition of the bars, even if the naming appears to be correct. Points to watch for are file or solder marks on the rivets which secure the bars to each other and to the suspender of the medal. Again, this test is not infallible since bars *do* occasionally work loose if subject to constant wear (particularly if the recipient was a cavalryman, for obvious reasons). But bars whose rivets appear to have been hammered should automatically be suspect, until a check of the medal roll passes them as authentic.

Examples of the earlier medals, particularly those to officers, may be found with unorthodox coupling of bars. Major L. L. Gordon, in his book *British Battles and Medals*, mentions a Naval General Service Medal, with bars for Guadeloupe and Anse la Barque in a large rectangular style which must have been quite unofficial. The medal is quite authentic, so it must be presumed that officers were allowed a certain degree of latitude in the manner in which they altered their medals.

The Man behind the Medal

With the collector of British campaign medals the person to whom the medal was awarded becomes almost as important as the medal itself. It is not sufficient to collect the medal and leave it at that. The collector must investigate it and delve into the archives to find out all that he can about the recipient. This can be a fascinating pastime and the value of the medal is greatly enhanced when the background to the award and the story of the man who won it can be ascertained. The Public Record Office and regimental museums have already been mentioned as useful sources of information, apart from the muster and medal rolls which only provide the bare details of the award.

In February 1966 Sotheby's of London auctioned an example of the Naval General Service Medal which fetched the incredible sum of £600. It was listed in the auction catalogue as follows:

> Naval General Service medal, 1793–1840, three bars, 4 June Boat Service, 1805, Emerald 13 March 1808, Basque Roads 1809, Edward Saurin, Lieut. R.N., *almost extremely fine and extremely rare.*
> 4th June, 1805 (Mid. 'Loire'), ten bars awarded; Emerald, 13th March, 1808 (Lieut.) twelve bars issued; Basque Roads, 1809 (Lieut 'Emerald'). For further details see O'Byrne, p. 1031.

'O'Byrne' is the name by which the *Naval Biographical Dictionary* compiled by William O'Byrne is familiarly known to naval historians. This encyclopaedic work, published in two volumes in 1849, was contemporaneous with the authorisation of the NGSM and is a most useful reference book, since it contains detailed biographies of officers of the Royal Navy, of the rank of lieutenant and above. The details of Edward Saurin, for example, occupy almost a whole column and from them we learn that he was the son of the Right Honourable William Saurin, Attorney-General for Ireland. He entered the Navy in August 1803 as a Volunteer on board the 36-gun *Euryalus* and served on the Irish station. In May 1804 he joined HMS *Loire* where he served as a Midshipman. O'Byrne then goes on:

'He was under fire, during that period, of the batteries in Mudros Bay, when they were gallantly stormed and carried, and the privateers *Confiance* and *Belier* taken, by the boats under the late Sir Jas. Lucas Yeo, 4 June, 1805.'

This gives the explanation for his Boat Service bar. O'Byrne then states that Saurin served in HMS *Emerald* under Captain F. L. Maitland, rising in rank from Midshipman to Master's Mate and then to Lieutenant in 1810. O'Byrne continues:

. . . contributed, on the night of 13 March, 1808, to the destruction in Vivero Harbour, of a large French schooner, *L'Apropos*, of 8 guns and 70 men';

To this is added a footnote:

'On this occasion he landed with a party under Lieut. Chas. Bertram, assisted in taking possession of a battery (whose guns, 8 24-pounders, were at the same time spiked) and, after having encountered and routed the crew, was for several hours engaged (under the annihilating fire of a body of troops not 30 yards distant) in a fruitless attempt to launch the schooner, which had been run on the rocks, and was in consequence set fire to and blown up.'

Details of this exploit were also given in *The London Gazette* (1808, page 416) while an interesting despatch from Captain Maitland to Admiral Lord Gardiner, written the following day, gives a most vivid account of this spirited action and is published in full under the entry for Maitland in John Marshall's *Royal Naval Biography*, published in 1824. The latter work only deals with officers of the rank of commander and above, but the despatch referred to mentions Mr. Saurin as a Master's Mate. By inference we learn that Saurin was not wounded on this occasion, though casualties were very heavy. Conversely, during an attack on the island of Lissa in May 1812, he was severely wounded. O'Byrne says that he lost his right arm, his left was shot through, his neckcloth was cut through the different folds and his sabre was broken by a ball. This boat action, in which 20 men serving under Saurin were killed, did not warrant the authorisation of a bar although it seems to have fulfilled the requirements for this, since Saurin was promoted to Commander on the strength of it.

His third bar was, in fact, gained as a Lieutenant aboard the *Emerald* in April 1809 when she was one of several ships present at the destruction of the French fleet in the Basque Roads. Subsequently Saurin was promoted to Captain in June 1814, but never served in an active capacity in this rank, remaining on half pay with a pension of £300 a year till he 'retired' in October 1846. He held the appointment of Commissioner of Stamps and Taxes for many years and, in July 1828, married Lady Mary Ryder, second daughter of the Earl of Harrowby. From the *Dictionary of National Biography* we glean the additional information that 'Admiral Edward Saurin died 28th February 1878, leaving a son, William Granville Saurin.'

Apart from the works of O'Byrne and Marshall, the earlier and later periods are respectively covered by Charnock's *Biographia Navalis* (published in three volumes between 1794 and 1798) and Clowes' *Royal Navy*.

The Army is not nearly so well served. Fortescue's thirteen-volume *History of the British Army* covers the period from 1660 to 1870 in some detail, but without the extensive biographical notes which distinguish the naval histories listed above. The gap is, however, filled to some extent by regimental histories and records, many of which have been published. Apart from medal and muster rolls most regimental museums will be found to contain documentary material, despatches, reports and diaries, relating to the actions in which the regiment has taken part, together with personal data concerning individual officers and men. There is no short cut to filling in the details of the personal history of the recipient of a medal or bar, but there can be no doubt that such background material adds greatly to the interest—and value—of the item. Such material as photographs or portraits of the recipient, or military items directly associated with him, should not be overlooked. These include documents like discharge papers, citations, correspondence and warrants for promotion in rank.

Medal Groups

The fact that British medals are usually named to the recipient means that they can be collected in groups. Certain groups are very common: Pip, Squeak and Wilfred—as the First World War trio of 1914–15 Star, British War Medal and Victory Medal are popularly known—form a very common group. Second World War groups exist, but since they do not have the name of the recipient these groups are of little or no interest as such. They only become interesting if they also include at least one medal bearing the name of the recipient (the Military General Service Medal, for example). The Queen's and King's medals for South Africa are another common group. Any additions to these common groups immediately add considerably to their interest and value. The addition of a gallantry award (see Chapter 4) or one of the miscellaneous types of medal, such as the Long Service and Good Conduct Medal, also enhances the value of a group.

I have illustrated a rather attractive group of seven medals which span a period of twenty years in the service of a soldier and illustrate the progress of his military career and the areas in which he fought. Yet one cannot get the whole story from the medals alone. 'They also serve who only stand and wait' is true of the modern Army, many of whose officers may have reached field rank without hearing a shot fired in anger and without receiving a single medal after more than twenty years' service. The medals were awarded to James D. Mackay who ran away from home at the age of fifteen to enlist in the Seaforth Highlanders in Edinburgh in 1880. During seventeen years of peacetime soldiering spent in Britain and Ireland he had advanced steadily in rank from private to sergeant-major, when his battalion was posted to Egypt. He took part in the campaign for the re-conquest of the Sudan in 1898 and fought with distinction at the Battle of Omdurman, for which he was subsequently commissioned in the Dublin Fusiliers. His first taste of service in Africa brought him the Queen's Sudan Medal and the Khedive's Medal, the latter with the bars for The Atbara and Khartoum (a fairly common combination).

A short time later he transferred to the Middlesex Regiment where he was promoted Lieutenant and returned to Africa, this time on secondment to the recently formed King's African Rifles, with whom he served intermittently up to the outbreak of the First World War. His service in this area earned him the African General Service Medal with four bars. The first of these, inscribed 'Jubaland', was awarded for service against the Ogaden Somalis in November 1900–April 1901. The campaign in Uganda in 1905 brought him the bar for 'East Africa 1905'. By now he had returned to the Seaforths as a captain and was seconded to the KAR for service in the Nandi country, recognised by the bar 'Nandi 1905–6'. The fourth bar, 'Somaliland 1908–10', was awarded for further services in that area against the forces of the Mad Mullah. During the Edwardian period Mackay served in Zanzibar where he organised the constabulary and taught the Sultan to drive a motor car! This service was recognised by the conferment upon him of the Star of Zanzibar.

The 1st Berkshire Regiment in action at the Battle of Tofrek in the Sudan in 1885

By the outbreak of the First World War he had been promoted to major and was again detached from his regiment to command native troops, this time against the forces of Colonel von Lettow-Vorbeck in German East Africa (Tanganyika). In 1915 he was promoted to lieutenant-colonel and subsequently was awarded the Distinguished Service Order and was Mentioned in Despatches (as indicated by the oak leaf on the Victory Medal). Service during the war brought him the conventional trio of the 1914–15 Star, the British War Medal and the Victory Medal, which complete this interesting group.

3 OTHER CAMPAIGN MEDALS

The award of campaign medals by other countries also developed in the nineteenth century. No country produced as many different medals as did Britain, but no other country was involved in so many wars and campaigns in so many parts of the world. Significantly the countries which came nearest to Britain in the number of medals they awarded were Russia and France, both of which expanded their colonial territories enormously during the nineteenth century.

Imperial Russia had one advantage over Britain in regard to the award of medals; it had a much wider range of decorations with which to award individual acts of heroism, and usually each decoration was divided into several classes, so that the choice was large. In many cases a decoration would have been given in cases where no distinctive campaign medal was struck. Nevertheless many of the wars involving Russian troops were honoured by a special medal. Among those which may be encountered are the medals for the Khiva campaign (1873), the Turkish War (1877–78) and the Japanese War (1904–5).

Russian medals have almost as great an antiquity as British medals, the earliest being the bronze oval medal awarded to those who took part in the capture of Kalish, Poland, on 18 October 1706. The obverse portrayed Tsar Peter the Great while the reverse showed him charging on horseback. The Northern War, which lasted from 1700 till 1721, resulted in numerous medals, often awarded in gold to officers and in silver or bronze to NCOs and enlisted men, and these are usually most attractively designed, with a profile of the Tsar on the obverse and an appropriate battle scene on the reverse. Medals were issued for the battles of Poltava (1709), Gangut (1714) and the Aland Islands (1720) as well as in commemoration of the Treaty of Nystad which brought this war between Russia and Sweden to an end. Subsequent medals marked the Battle of Kunersdorf in the Seven Years War (1760), the Battle of Kagul in the Turkish War of 1768–74, the naval victory at Tchesme in 1770, the Battles of Kinburn and Ochakoff in the Russo-Turkish War of 1787–91 and the Swedish War of 1788–90. After that there were numerous medals for service against the Poles, the Turks, the Swedes and the French. There were medals for award to Persians who helped Russia to 'liberate' the Caucasus from Turkey. Although Russia and Turkey were deadly enemies for most of the nineteenth century it is interesting to note that the Mouraviev Medal of 1834 was awarded for service with the Russian expedition against Mehemet Ali of Egypt who was rebelling against the Sultan of Turkey. Another unusual medal was that awarded to all officers and men who took part in the campaign of 1848–49 to suppress the rebellion in Hungary and Transylvania. The rebels tried to win independence for Hungary against the Austrian Habsburgs who retaliated by calling on their Russian ally to invade the country and pacify it. The use of Russian troops in this way had a strange parallel in the Hungarian Uprising of 1956.

Many so-called campaign medals of Russia were purely commemorative in nature, and were awarded to officers and men who happened to be

Nicholas I awarded many commemorative medals which had the same status as campaign medals

facing page Hitler awarded campaign medals to his invading armies in his various acquisitions of land before the declaration of war. Here Nazi troops march through the streets of Prague

serving in the army at a particular time. There were medals to celebrate the 50th anniversary of the defence of Sebastopol in the Crimean War (1904) and the bicentenary of the Battle of Poltava (1909), not to mention medals celebrating the tercentenary of the Romanov Dynasty (1913) and even a medal awarded by Tsar Nicholas I in 1842 to members of the Sixth Royal Prussian Cuirassier Regiment to celebrate the 25th anniversary of his appointment as honorary colonel of the regiment. Not to be outdone, King Frederick William IV of Prussia awarded gold or gilt-bronze medals to more than 3,000 Russian soldiers the following year to commemorate the 25th anniversary of his appointment as honorary colonel of the Fifth Russian Kaluga Infantry Regiment!

A curious feature of Russian campaign medals is that no distinctive ribbons were produced. The ribbons of existing decorations were used, either on their own or in combination with the ribbons of other decorations.

During the First World War a large number of medals were awarded under the Provisional Government (July-November 1917), but their exact status has never been established. At least eleven different medals are known to exist, with portraits of leading generals, allegorical subjects symbolising victory and warlike slogans. Some of them were undoubtedly given to troops for military service, but others may only have been souvenirs designed to boost morale.

Under the Soviet regime numerous orders and decorations have been awarded, many of them being given for service in particular campaigns rather than as awards for individual acts of gallantry. In addition there were a large number of campaign medals for the Second World War—or Great Patriotic War of 1941–45 as it is known in Russia. These include medals for the defence of Leningrad, Stalingrad and other important cities, the capture of Berlin, Vienna and other leading enemy cities, and the liberation of Belgrade, Warsaw and Prague. One of the most coveted medals is the rather crude bronze medal awarded by the All Russian Central Committee to those who took part in the storming of the Winter Palace on 17 October 1917 which began the Revolution.

No campaign medals have been awarded to Soviet personnel since the end of the Second World War, though the tradition of issuing medals celebrating important anniversaries has been continued. Among the more recent issues may be mentioned the bronze medal marking the twentieth anniversary of victory in the Second World War,

awarded to all officers and men who served in the war and were still on active service in 1965. All medals and decorations from 1920 onwards have had distinctive ribbons.

France

Until Napoleon came to power outstanding military service was rewarded by the presentation of special swords, muskets or other weapons. The *Légion d'Honneur* was instituted in 1802 and bestowed on men for distinguished military or civil service. No attempt was made, however, to authorise medals to denote service in particular campaigns. The award of such medals was curiously similar to that in Britain, for it was not until 1857 that anything was done to reward those who had served in the campaigns from 1792 till 1815. The revival of interest in the former glories of France, fostered by the Emperor Napoleon III after he seized power in 1853, included the St. Helena Medal, instituted in 1857 and given to all soldiers and sailors surviving from the era of the Napoleonic Wars. The bronze medal bore the effigy of Napoleon I on the obverse, while the reverse was inscribed in French signifying 'Campaigns of 1792–1815 to his Companions of Glory, his last Thought. Saint Helena 5 May 1821'. The date is that of Napoleon's death. The green and red ribbon of this medal was revived in 1915 for use with the *Croix de Guerre* of the First World War.

French personnel who served in the war of 1854–56 against Russia were given the British Crimean and Baltic Medals, bestowed by Queen Victoria. Unofficial bars were manufactured in France for Tracktir, Kinburn, Mamelon Vert and Malakoff. Napoleon III's campaigns in Italy in 1859 resulted in a silver medal with bars commemorating Magenta, Solferino and other battles. A China Medal was given in 1861 to those who took part in the Anglo-French Expedition to China in 1860. Napoleon's ill-fated Mexican Expedition of 1862–63 also resulted in a campaign medal with appropriate engagement bars. French troops who took part in the defence of Rome against the Italians in 1867 were awarded a Pontifical Cross by Pope Pius IX. Special medals were awarded for service in Tonkin (1883–93), Madagascar (1885 and 1894–95), Dahomey (1892) and Morocco (1909), as well as a Colonial Medal (1893) corresponding to the British general service medals and awarded for service in many different parts of the world. The medal was made retrospective, going as far back as the Algiers Expedition of 1830.

Napoleon I instituted the *Legion d'Honneur* for distinguished services to France but it was Napoleon III who issued a medal to commemorate the Napoleonic wars, *and left* Maximilian of Austria was the first and last Emperor of Mexico. He was shot by Mexican republicans in 1867

The same medal has continued in use up to the present day and includes bars for service in Indochina and the Far East in the 1950s.

Service in the Franco-Prussian War was belatedly recognised by a bronze medal, given to survivors of that war in 1911. The First World War was remembered by a medal depicting the helmeted figure of France. There was also a medal awarded to victims of the German invasion, with bars signifying 'Hostage of War' or 'Political Prisoner'. In addition the inter-allied Victory Medal, with suitable French inscriptions, was also awarded.

A *Médaille du Levant* (Levant Medal) was instituted in 1922 for service in Syria and Cilicia after the First World War. The Vichy government re-issued this medal with the bar 'Levant 1941' for those who resisted the British invasion of Syria in the Second World War. In the Twenties several other medals appeared which commemorated service in the First World War. They included medals for the Dardanelles Expedition, for escaped prisoners and for combatant volunteers. Several of these 'special service' medals were revived for award after the Second World War.

The Second World War resulted in a fine crop of medals. These included the Liberation Cross and medals for the Resistance, the Free French Forces, ex-prisoners, deportees and civilian wounded. A bronze hexagonal medal commemorated the war itself and a medal was struck to mark service in the Italian campaign. Like Britain, France issued a medal in 1952 for service in the Korean War.

above, left The obverse of the Liberation Order, France World War II. The ribbon is black-edged green with two thin green stripes. *right* The obverse of the Medal for Service with Free French Forces, World War II. The ribbon is blue with diagonal pink stripes.

below, left The obverse of the Resistance Medal –France, World War II. It has a pink-edged and striped black ribbon. *middle* The obverse of the Medal for Déportation for Acts of Resistance – France World War II. It has a vertically striped blue and white pink-edged ribbon. *right* The obverse of the Medal for Internment for Acts of Resistance – France World War II. It has a diagonally striped blue and white pink-edged ribbon

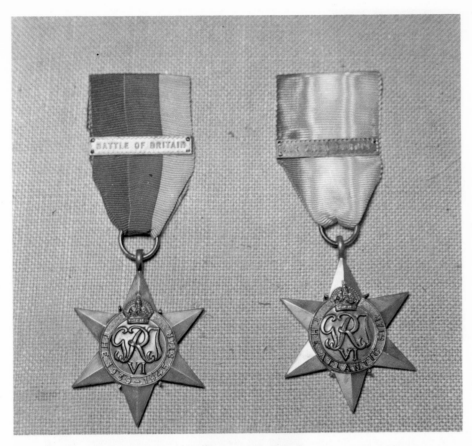

left The obverse of the 1939-45 Star and the Atlantic Star. The 1939-45 Star has the much prized Battle of Britain bar, while the Atlantic Star has a bar for the Air Crew Europe Star

right The obverse of the Air Crew Europe Star which has a bar, the France and Germany Star, and the Africa Star which has bars for 8th Army, North Africa 1942-43 and 1st Army

The American Medal for Merit – Civilian division is awarded for outstanding services to the country

The Order of St. Olaf which is a Norwegian order. St. Olaf was King in the ninth century and converted Norway to Christianity

Theodore Roosevelt instituted various campaign medals when he discovered that, as commander-in-chief of the United States Army, he was entitled to do so

United States of America

The United States was very slow to introduce campaign medals for service in the many wars involving its soldiers and sailors. Nothing was done about this until the Spanish-American War of 1898 when Congress authorised a bronze medal to be presented to all officers and men who took part in the Battle of Manila Bay on 1 May of that year. The medal is popularly known as the Dewey Medal, since it bears a profile of Commodore George Dewey on the obverse. A similar medal, for service in the West Indies, was approved by Congress in 1901 and is known as the Sampson Medal, from the effigy of Admiral William T. Sampson which appears on the obverse. An interesting feature of this medal was the brooch at the top of the ribbon on which was inscribed the name of the recipient's ship. Bars for no fewer than 47 different engagements or skirmishes between 27 April and 14 August 1898 were issued with

this medal. The crews of 68 ships received this medal, some with as many as six or seven bars. In January 1905 the services of the Army were recognised by the Spanish Campaign Medal (1898) and the Philippine Campaign Medal (1899–1906), the latter being intended for service in various expeditions against the Filipinos who, having ejected the Spaniards, were none too happy to find themselves under American occupation. Both of these medals were subsequently authorised for award to naval and Marine Corps personnel who served ashore in the respective campaigns.

The year 1905 was a great one for catching up on previous wars. A medal was also introduced that year for award to Army personnel who took part in the relief expedition to China in 1900 at the time of the Boxer Rebellion. Naval personnel became eligible for this award in 1908. It was brought to the attention of President Theodore Roosevelt that, in his capacity as Commander-in-Chief he was empowered to authorise 'badges' to be worn as part of the uniform of officers and men who had served in various campaigns. Though this was primarily concerned with the recent conflicts in the Philippines, the West Indies and China, President Roosevelt took the opportunity to examine the situation for earlier campaigns. As a result two further medals were introduced. A medal portraying Abraham Lincoln was awarded to veterans of the Union forces in the Civil War of 1861–65, and a medal featuring an Indian warrior on horseback was given to veterans of the Indian wars from 1865 till 1891. A Civil War Medal depicting the famous battle between the warships *Monitor* and *Merrimac* was instituted in 1908 for the Navy and Marine Corps. Two versions of this medal, differing in the arm of the services of the recipient, were produced.

Having made a late start with campaign medals the United States soon caught up with Britain and Russia. In the period before America entered the First World War in 1917 there were medals for the occupation of Cuba and Porto Rico, for the pacification of Cuba and for the campaigns in Nicaragua, Mexico, Haiti and Santo Domingo. There were also medals indicating service in the Spanish War, the Philippines or on the Mexican border where the applicants did not qualify for existing medals because they had not been actively engaged in battle. Only one medal was issued for the First World War and that was the Allied Victory Medal. Possibly on account of its late entry into the war the United States found it practicable to issue engagement bars with this medal—nineteen clasps for the Army and nineteen for the Navy and Marine Corps. In addition, however, the latter services were also eligible for ten of the bars on the Army list. Originally a small silver star was awarded with the Victory Medal and worn on the ribbon to indicate a citation for gallantry (similar to the British oak leaf for a Mention in Despatches), but this was later replaced by the separate award known as the Silver Star.

In the period between the World Wars the United States awarded campaign medals for service in Germany (1918–23), Nicaragua (1926–33), the Yangtse (1926–32) and China (1937–39). The American equivalent of the British general service medals were the Navy and Marine Corps Expeditionary Medals introduced in 1926 for award to personnel who served in various expeditions and minor campaigns as far back as Panama, 1873. The bars issued with these medals indicate how far-flung American interests were in the nineteenth and early twentieth centuries—Hawaii (1874), Samoa (1888), Korea (1894), Syria (1903) and Russia (1905) among many others. Postwar bars included those for service in Siberia (1920) and Honduras (1924). The last bar awarded to these medals was a silver 'W', given to Navy and Marine Corps personnel who defended Wake Island against Japanese attack from 7 December to 22 December 1941.

Inevitably the Second World War resulted in a large number of medals. The first of these, the Defense Service Medal, was awarded for service in the period *before* the United States entered the war and covered the period during the state of emergency proclaimed on 8 September 1939 up to the time of Japanese attack on Pearl Harbour on 7 December 1941.

The first campaign medals of the war itself were instituted in 1942 and covered the European-African-Middle Eastern Campaign, the Asiatic-Pacific Campaign and the American Campaign, the last-named indicating combat service in the American theatre of operations outside the mainland of the United States. A Victory Medal was authorised in July 1945 and an Army of Occupation Medal, for postwar service in Germany and Japan, in 1946. In addition, however, there were Unit Citations for the Army and Navy, the Navy Unit Commendation and several different medals, bars and citations for the Merchant Marine. Since the Second World War there have been medals for National Defence Service, Korea and Indochina, in addition to a host of gallantry and meritorious service awards which are dealt with in the next chapter.

Germany

Prior to 1918 every kingdom, grand-duchy and principality of the German Empire produced its own medals and decorations so that, although the actual number of wars fought by Germany was small, the total output of medals was enormous. Medals were struck by various German states in connection with the Danish War of 1863–64, the Seven Weeks War of 1866 and the Franco-German War of 1870–71 as well as the First World War itself.

Service in the First World War was belatedly recognised by the Cross of Honour, instituted by President Hindenburg in July 1934. The cross was made of bronzed iron, with crossed swords for combatants. Crosses given to widows and parents of recipients killed in action were covered with black lacquer. After the Nazis came to power in 1933 they celebrated the tenth anniversary of the

top, left to right
The obverse of the Medal of the Army of Occupation in Germany – U.S.A. 1918-23. It has a black, white, red and blue striped ribbon
The obverse and reverse of the Nazi Union of Sudetenland with the Third Reich Medal. The bar was given for service in the Protectorate of Bohemia and Moravia in 1939. It has a black ribbon with central red stripe
The obverse and reverse of the Nazi Defence Wall or Western Wall Medal. It has a brown ribbon with two white stripes
below The obverse and reverse of the Nazi Ostmedaille or Winter Battle in the East Medal. It has a red ribbon with white and black centre stripes

unsuccessful uprising of 1923 by issuing the Blood Order to all those who had taken part in the Munich *putsch*.

The distinction between decorations for gallantry and medals for campaign service is difficult in the case of certain German awards. The Iron Cross, for example, was originally intended as a decoration for valour on the field of battle but became debased in both World Wars by virtue of its award to almost every soldier who saw action. In the same way the War Merit Cross instituted during the Second World War is about as common as the British War Medal, though originally designed as a lower award than the Iron Cross. The Cross of Honour for the Spanish Civil War had four classes and of these the bronze or fourth class was regarded virtually as a campaign medal for personnel who served with the Nazi Condor Legion on the side of Franco during the war of 1936–39.

Two other prewar medals are worthy of note. The Anschluss Medal was given to troops who took part in the invasion of Austria in March 1938 and the Sudetenland Medal went to those who invaded Czechoslovakia in October 1938. A variation of this medal was the Protectorate Medal, awarded to troops involved in the second invasion of Czechoslovakia, in March 1939, which resulted in the establishment of the German Protectorate of Bohemia and Moravia.

During the Second World War medals were struck for the Russian campaign of 1941–42 and for service on the West Wall (Siegfried Line) in the defence of Germany. The Luftschutz Medal was awarded to personnel in the civil defence and fire services. After the war the wearing of Nazi

medals was forbidden, but in 1957 the Federal
Republic permitted the wearing of such medals,
providing that the Nazi swastika emblem was
removed. As a result many of the Second World
War medals have now been re-issued in a modified
form.

Italy

Like Germany, Italy had several gallantry awards
which were distributed almost as freely as campaign medals and, in some cases, were produced
for specific campaigns. Perhaps the best known
of these is the Medal for Military Valour, instituted by the Kingdom of Sardinia in 1833. A
special version of this silver medal, inscribed
SPEDIZIONE D'ORIENTE (Eastern Expedition),
was struck in honour of the Sardinian contingent
who fought alongside the British, French and
Turks in the Crimea. Some 450 officers and men of
the British Army were given this medal in recognition of outstanding services. Specially inscribed
versions of this medal were awarded to Cara-
binieri who fought in the Abyssinian campaign
of 1936 and there was a war cross for distinguished
service in the Spanish Civil War.

The campaign medals, as such, date from 1859
when Napoleon III gave a silver medal to the
Italian troops under his command. Other medals
connected with the campaigns for the unification
of Italy were the United Italy Medal (1848–70) and
the Garibaldi Medal, struck in 1860. Campaign
medals were later issued in connection with the
African expeditions of 1891–96, the Boxer Rebellion in China (1900) and the war with Turkey in
1911. Silver medals were awarded to personnel
(including many British sailors) who assisted the
injured after the earthquakes of Messina (1908)
and Avezzano (1915). The First World War was
marked by the War Medal and the Allied Victory
Medal.

The ambitions of Mussolini to create a new
Roman Empire resulted in medals for the Abyssinian campaign (1935–36), four different campaign awards for service in the Spanish Civil War
(1936–39), the invasion of Albania in 1939, the
campaign against France (1940), the campaigns
against Greece and Yugoslavia and the occupation
of Dalmatia (all 1941) and the African campaign
(1940–43). The last of these medals was inscribed
in both Italian and German and featured a
triumphal arch flanked by the Italian fasces and
the German swastika. The reverse showed two
knights in armour standing on a helpless crocodile

The obverse and reverse of the Italian Africa Campaign Medal,
which in fact was never issued. It has a white ribbon, with
centre red stripe and black left edge

Hitler and Mussolini at the 'Wolf's Lair' in 1942. Mussolini much admired this almost impregnable retreat

(the British Empire) and forcibly closing its jaws (the Suez Canal). It is thought that this medal was to have been issued after the Germans and Italians had driven the British out of Egypt. The Allied victory at El Alamein, however, put paid to this hope and the medal was never issued. The ship which was bringing the medals from Italy to North Africa was sunk by Allied aircraft in Bizerta Harbour. When the Allies captured Bizerta in May 1943 the medals were salvaged from the sunken wreck and subsequently fell into the hands of souvenir hunters. After the Second World War three medals were awarded for war service to mark the liberation of Italy and for service in the partisan forces (Volunteers for Liberty). In addition there were numerous Fascist medals, the most important of which was instituted by Mussolini for those who took part in the Fascist March on Rome in October 1922.

Japan

The last of the major belligerents in the two World Wars, Japan, has also produced a number of campaign medals. The earliest of these were all issued in connection with service in wars against China, in 1874, 1894–95 and the Boxer Rebellion of 1900. Subsequently medals were produced for the Russo-Japanese War of 1904–5 and the annexation of Korea in 1912. One of the two Japanese medals for the First World War was the Allied Victory Medal suitably inscribed. The other medal—an ironic award in view of subsequent history—had a blue and white ribbon and was given for service against Germany. The Japanese were mainly responsible for the defeat of German forces at Tsingtau and Kiautschou in the early months of the war. Medals were awarded to troops who took part in the campaigns in Manchuria

Debris in the streets of Dublin
during the Easter Rebellion of 1916
and soldiers on patrol. The
rebellion was put down most
brutally

(1931–34) and China (1937), but the events of Hiroshima and Nagasaki overtook the Japanese Empire before medals for the campaigns of the Second World War could be issued.

Other Countries

Most countries, at some time or another, have been involved in wars or national emergencies for which medals have been produced. The Irish Republic, for example, instituted medals in 1942 for men who fought the British in the Easter Rising of 1916 and the 'Troubles' which ensued between that date and 1921. Ironically, 1916–21 medals had a ribbon of black and tan colouring—a grim reference to the Black and Tans, the British irregular forces who served in Ireland during that period. In addition the Irish government issued service medals to the military forces and Merchant Navy who served during the period from 1939 to 1946, even though Ireland remained neutral throughout the Second World War.

Many countries produced campaign medals for the First World War. Belgium instituted the Yser Medal and the *Croix du Feu* (cross of fire), as well as special awards to seamen, civilian volunteers, social workers, women, political prisoners, deportees, troops of the African campaign and other parts of the colonies, as well as the Victory Medal and a commemorative war medal. Czechoslovakia awarded the Revolutionary Cross to all those who served with the Czecho-Slovak Legions in France, Italy and Russia during and after the war. Luxembourg had a Volunteers Medal for those who served in the war; this medal was revived for the Second World War. Portugal issued medals for overseas service, a wounded medal and the Allied Victory Medal. For service in the Second World War campaign medals were awarded by Denmark, Norway, Greece, the Netherlands,

The obverse of the Service Medal, 1917-21 of Eire. It has a halved black and tan ribbon in reference to the British irregular forces of that period

Poland and Yugoslavia, in addition to those countries already mentioned. In several cases special medals for service in the partisans or resistance movements were produced.

Apart from the two World Wars several minor wars have resulted in campaign medals. The war between Poland and Soviet Russia in 1918–21 was commemorated by a medal struck by the Poles, who also awarded a medal to those troops who served under General Zeligowski in Central Lithuania in 1920–22. Spain produced numerous medals in connection with the Civil War of 1936–39, while earlier medals marked service in the Civil War of 1873–74 and campaigns in Cuba, the Philippines and Morocco. Denmark awarded a medal in 1920 to members of the Allied Commission who served in Slesvig during the period of the plebiscite, when the inhabitants voted for the inclusion of their territory in Germany or Denmark.

Since the Second World War the unsettled state of the world has been reflected in the medals issued by Israel and the Arab countries in connection with the wars of 1948, 1956 and 1967. A number of campaign medals have been issued, under the auspices of the United Nations, for service with custodian forces in Cyprus, the Congo, Gaza, and other trouble spots, as well as the well-known Korea Medal already mentioned.

In general campaign medals of other countries lack the personnel interest of British awards since they seldom bear the names of the recipients. Moreover information about them, and the circumstances in which they were awarded, is often hard to find and this explains why they are not so popular with collectors. Nevertheless they are often attractively designed and all of them, in some way, tell a story of hardship and fortitude, of action and adventure, and represent tiny fragments of living history.

below, left to right
The obverse of the Siamese or Thai War Medal of 1917-18. It has a purple ribbon with two narrow black stripes
The obverse of the Siamese Victory Medal of 1918. It was the country's medal design but has the same rainbow-coloured ribbon as the other Allies medals.
The obverse of the Korean Memorial Medal of Ethiopia. It has a red, yellow, green, blue and white ribbon.
The obverse of the Combat Medal of North Korea which was awarded during the Korean War

John Cornwall of H M S *Lancaster* who won the VC during the Battle of Jutland aged 15. He is the youngest person ever to have won it

4 GALLANTRY AWARDS

Medals and crosses for brave conduct in action are of comparatively recent origin. Mention has already been made of individual awards made to soldiers during the Civil War of 1642–49. In the latter half of the seventeenth century there were several cases of medals awarded for gallantry. After the Battle of La Hogue in 1692, for example, a gold medal was awarded to Captain John Tupper for distinguished conduct. Captain Peter Joliffe and William Thompson received similar medals in 1694 and 1695 respectively for outstanding exploits against French ships. Throughout the eighteenth century there are records of individual awards of gold medals and chains to naval officers in recognition of their exploits in various sea battles and it is probable that these precedents led to the introduction of the Navy Gold Medal for the Glorious First of June (1794) and the subsequent naval gold medals of the Napoleonic Wars.

Second Lieutenant Charles Hazlitt Upham of the New Zealand armed forces was the only man to win the VC twice during World War II

This Victoria Cross was awarded to Sergeant-Major Peter Gill of the Loodiana regiment for his bravery in saving three people on 4 June 1857 during the Indian Mutiny

It was many years later, however, before Britain instituted decorations for bravery, as opposed to distinguished service or campaign service. The earliest attempt to do so was the Meritorious Service Medal, established in 1845 and originally awarded to sergeants of the Army for distinguished service and individual acts of bravery. This medal was superseded as a bravery award in 1854 by the Distinguished Conduct Medal which remains to this day as an important decoration to NCOs and enlisted men of the Army. The Meritorious Service Medal, on the other hand, is also still in existence, but is now awarded to NCOs and warrant officers for meritorious service.

Forty years after the Napoleonic Wars the peace of Europe was again seriously disturbed, this time by war between Russia and Turkey. Britain, France and Sardinia became involved on the side of Turkey in a war which was fought mainly in the Crimea. The war began in September 1854 and came to an end in March 1856. Queen Victoria was deeply concerned at the hardships endured by her troops in the Crimea and took a keen personal interest in their welfare and morale. The idea of a medal for outstanding acts of bravery is said to have been raised by the Prince Consort. The Queen welcomed the idea and in February 1856 the establishment of the Victoria Cross was announced. The first investiture was held in Hyde Park, London on 26 June 1857 when 62 of the original recipients received this highly coveted decoration.

The Victoria Cross, a cross pattee made from bronze taken from a gun captured at Sebastopol, bears the crown and British lion and the words FOR VALOUR. It is suspended by a ring through the letter V and has ornamental bars at both ends of the ribbon. Originally a blue ribbon was worn with naval crosses and a crimson one with army crosses, but in the First World War crimson was adopted as the ribbon for the Navy as well. When the ribbon is worn on its own a tiny replica of the cross is attached to the ribbon.

The Victoria Cross is awarded to servicemen regardless of rank and it takes precedence over all other British orders and decorations. The award of the VC also carries a pension; originally this was fixed at £10, but in 1898 it could be raised to as much as £50 if the recipient was poor, and in 1959 it was raised to £100 for all surviving recipients, irrespective of their circumstances. The cross was awarded for bravery in the face of the enemy, but on six occasions it has been given for acts of bravery not in the face of the enemy, five of these awards being to a surgeon and four privates of the 24th Foot (South Wales Borderers) for saving the lives of their comrades in a shipwreck off the Andaman Islands in May 1867. In 1858 the cross was extended to civilians. Three magistrates were awarded the VC during the Indian Mutiny and a fourth during the Afghan War. Nowadays civilians would be given the George Cross, instituted as the civilian equivalent of the VC.

Women are eligible for the VC but so far no woman has won it. Considerable controversy was raised because Odette Hallowes and Violette Szabo were awarded the GC instead of the VC for courageous acts in the face of the enemy during the Second World War. Posthumous awards were not made until 1902. Officers and men who were nominated for the VC but died in action or from their wounds did not receive the cross, though the award was listed in *The London Gazette*. King Edward VII decided that the VC should be given to relatives of dead recipients and this was made retrospective, right back to the Crimean War. In the 116 years since the institution of this decoration 1,348 crosses have been awarded, not counting the three occasions on which men have won a bar to the cross for subsequent acts of bravery. Captain Martin Leake won the VC in the Boer War and received a bar for gallantry in France in November 1914. Captain Chevasse was awarded the VC for bravery at Guillemont on 9 August 1916 and again for services at Wieltje, Belgium on 2 August 1917. Second Lieutenant C. H. Upham of the New Zealand military forces won his first VC in Crete in May 1941 and his second in the Western Desert in July 1942.

Bravery runs in families and there are several cases of families boasting of more than one holder of the VC. Three cases occurred where father and son both won the VC. Lord Roberts won the VC as a lieutenant during the Indian Mutiny while his son, Lieutenant the Hon. F. H. S. Roberts won it posthumously during the Boer War. Captain W. N. Congreve won the VC in 1899 during the Boer War and his son, Brevet Major W. Congreve, won it in France in 1916. Major C. J. S. Gough won his cross during the Indian Mutiny while his son Brevet Major J. E. Gough won the VC in the Somaliland campaign of 1903. Four sets of brothers won the VC. Major C. J. S. Gough, already mentioned, and his brother, Lieutenant H. H. Gough, both won the cross during the Indian Mutiny—a unique instance of three VCs in one

Captain N G Chevasse of the Royal Army Medical Corps who won the VC twice and died of his wounds during World War I

family. Major R. W. Sartorius and his brother Captain E. H. Sartorius both won the VC in 1874, in the Ashanti campaign and Afghanistan respectively. Second Lieutenant A. B. Turner won the VC in France in 1915 while his brother, Major V. B. Turner gained the award in the Western Desert in 1942. Lieutenant-Colonel R. B. Bradford won the VC in France in 1916 while his brother, Lieutenant-Commander G. N. Bradford received it for bravery at Zeebrugge in 1918.

Of the 1,348 crosses, 111 were awarded during the Crimean and Baltic campaigns of 1854–56, 182 for the Indian Mutiny, 78 for the Boer War, 633 for the First World War, 182 for the Second World War and 4 for Korea. In the minor campaigns of the period up to the outbreak of the First World War a further 151 crosses were awarded. Five VCs were awarded in the period between the World Wars and one VC, to Lance Corporal Rambahadur Limbu of the Gurkhas, has been awarded for service against terrorists in Sarawak (1966). All four crosses awarded in Vietnam (1966–69) went to Australian infantrymen serving alongside the American and South Vietnamese forces and two of these were posthumous. From these statistics it will be noted that the VC has become much rarer in recent years; in fact as many crosses were awarded in the Indian Mutiny as in the Second World War. The sole reason for this is that, until 1914, the VC was virtually the only decoration which could be awarded and in many cases a lesser award might have been made had it been available.

Nevertheless, two other gallantry awards were instituted at the time of the Crimean War. The Distinguished Conduct Medal replaced the Meritorious Service Medal in 1854 as a gallantry award for NCOs and men in the Army. The following year the Conspicuous Gallantry Medal was instituted for petty officers and seamen of the Navy. The DCM has been in use continuously since that date, but the CGM was discontinued after the Crimean War (in which ten men received the award) and revived in 1874. Of all the British gallantry awards it is the rarest, no more than 233 having been given since 1874.

Acts of bravery and distinguished service in action by officers of the Army and Navy were rewarded by appointment as Companions of various orders of chivalry (see Chapter 6), but it was felt that these awards should be confined to distinguished service over a longer period. The Distinguished Service Order (despite its name) was introduced in 1886 mainly to reward officers

The obverse of the Distinguished Conduct Medal which was established in 1854. It has a red ribbon with black centre stripe

Conspicuous Gallantry Medals showing *left* Original ribbon; blue with white central stripe. *centre* New ribbon of 1921; dark blue-edged white. *right* Ribbon for the R.A.F.; dark blue-edged light blue

A captured German machine gun post being used by the British in 1918 during the Battle of the Marne. Many MC's were won by people who captured such posts

below, top row, left to right
The obverse of the Military Cross which was instituted on 31 December 1914. It has a white ribbon with central purple stripe
The Distinguished Service Cross was originally called the Conspicuous Service Cross. It is given to naval officers and has a dark blue ribbon with central light blue stripe

bottom row, left to right
The Distinguished Flying Cross was instituted in 1918 as an equivalent for the R.A.F. of the Military Cross and Distinguished Service Cross. It has a violet and white diagonally striped ribbon
The Air Force Cross is given for bravery in the air but not in active service against the enemy. It has a diagonally striped crimson and white ribbon

for acts of gallantry which were not quite in the same class as deeds for which the Victoria Cross would be merited. Up to the First World War the DSO was awarded to officers of any rank, but after the introduction of the Military Cross in 1914 it tended to be confined to officers of the rank of major and above (or the equivalent ranks in the Navy and the Air Force). However there are a few cases, from the Second World War and other campaigns of more recent times, in which junior officers have received the DSO for conduct which was felt to deserve more than the MC but not the VC. The DSO is in white enamel with gilt edges and bears the royal monogram in the centre.

The Military Cross was instituted on 31 December 1914 for award to Army officers (captains and subalterns) and warrant officers. In 1931 the award of the MC was extended to majors. A decoration for junior naval officers was the Conspicuous Service Cross, established in 1901. The name of this decoration was changed in October 1914 to the Distinguished Service Cross. Since 1931 this decoration has also been awarded to officers of the Merchant Navy. The Royal Air Force equivalent of the DSC and MC is the Distinguished Flying Cross, established in June 1918 following the formation of the RAF as a separate branch of the armed forces. Another RAF award, instituted at the same time, is the Air Force Cross, awarded for bravery in the air though not in active operations against the enemy. The ribbons of the DFC and the AFC differ from those of Army and Navy awards in that they have diagonal stripes of violet and crimson respectively.

The corresponding gallantry awards for NCOs and enlisted men of the three services were also introduced during the First World War. The

top row left to right (this page)
The obverse and reverse of the Distinguished Flying Medal
which has a purple and white diagonally-striped ribbon
The obverse and reverse of the Air Force Medal which has a
diagonally striped crimson and white ribbon
The Royal Red Cross is one of the few awards for women only.
This is a First Class with Bar. It has a blue-edged red ribbon

bottom row, left to right (this page)
The Distinguished Service Medal was founded in
1914 and has a blue ribbon with two white strips
The obverse of the Military Medal which was founded in 1916.
It has a blue, white and red ribbon.

Distinguished Service Medal, for petty officers and seamen, was established in October 1914, while the Military Medal appeared in March 1916. The Distinguished Flying Medal and Air Force Medal came into being in 1918. An Air Force version of the CGM was instituted in 1943 and differs from its Naval equivalent solely in its ribbon which is light blue with dark blue edges whereas the naval CGM has a white ribbon with dark blue edges—the same ribbon having been used for the Naval General Service Medal of Victorian times.

Various other decorations have been instituted in Britain and the Commonwealth. The Royal Red Cross was founded in 1883 as an award to women only and was given for distinguished nursing service with the armed forces. Awards to civilians for bravery began in 1866 when Queen Victoria instituted the Albert Medals for saving life on land or sea. The medals were awarded in gold or silver. The earliest medals were awarded for saving life in shipwrecks and other accidents at sea, but in 1877 similar medals for life-saving on land were introduced. These medals are now confined to posthumous awards. When the Order of the British Empire (see Chapter 6) was instituted in 1917 a medal, known as the British Empire Medal, was also established. At first this medal was given for individual acts of bravery, as well as distinguished service, by civilians, but in 1922 a separate gallantry award was instituted and was known as the Empire Gallantry Medal. The BEM was henceforth confined to awards for meritorious service, although in recent years it has been revived as a lesser gallantry award for civilians or military personnel for bravery not in

the face of the enemy. Where the BEM is now awarded for gallantry a cluster of silver oak leaves is worn on the ribbon.

The Empire Gallantry Medal was abolished in 1940 and replaced by the George Cross. Holders of the EGM exchanged their award for the GC which, since that date, is regarded as the civilian counterpart of the VC. For acts of bravery which were considered to be not quite so outstanding, the George Medal is awarded. Both the cross and the medal depict St. George and the Dragon. Strictly speaking the GC is awarded for bravery in cases where purely military honours would not be applicable. It was awarded to British agents who worked behind the enemy lines in the Second World War and has also been awarded to military personnel for such acts as bomb disposal where the enemy was not actually present. The George Cross was awarded to the people of Malta for their gallant defence of the island in the Second World War. The MBE (Member of the Order of the British Empire) is sometimes conferred as a gallantry award to officers of the armed forces and, like the gallantry award of the BEM, is signified by silver oak leaves on the ribbon.

The Indian Order of Merit was founded in 1837 for rewarding acts of bravery by officers and men of the Indian Army. Originally there were three classes of this order, but the highest class was abolished in 1912 when the award of the VC was extended to the Indian Army. This gallantry award was withdrawn from use in 1947 when India became an independent country. Gallantry awards have also been established at various times for the police, the fire service and the colonial service.

top row, left to right
The two Albert Medals for saving life on land (red) or at sea (blue). They have a red and white or blue and white ribbon respectively
The reverse of the British Empire Medal which was established in 1917. It has a pink ribbon with grey edges and a centre stripe
The George Cross is the premier civilian award for bravery and was established in 1940. It has a dark blue ribbon

bottom row, left to right
The reverse of the Empire Gallantry Medal which was established in 1922
The reverse of the George Medal which depicts St. George and the Dragon. It has a pink ribbon with five narrow blue stripes

Other Countries

As in Britain, medals were bestowed on people for acts of bravery on an individual basis but it was not until the Napoleonic Wars that these awards were instituted on a regular basis. Napoleon himself set the precedent for later awards by instituting the *Légion d'Honneur* in May 1802 while his army lay at Boulogne, waiting for the orders to invade England. The *Légion d'Honneur* served two purposes; it could be awarded for bravery in action or for twenty years' distinguished military or civilian service in peacetime. This remained the only French gallantry award until 1852 when the Military Medal was instituted. This decoration, known in French as the *Médaille Militaire*, is only awarded to the highest ranking officers (generals in command of armies or admirals commanding fleets) and NCOs and enlisted men for conspicuous gallantry in action. It therefore combines the functions of the British VC and such orders as Knight Commander of the Bath (see Chapter 6). The *Croix de Guerre* (war cross) was introduced in 1915, for award to officers and men of the armed forces. This award was re-introduced in the Second World War, with a different ribbon. The *Croix de Guerre* is worn with a wide variety of different emblems on the ribbon, ranging from a bronze star for a mention in regimental despatches to a laurel branch for mention in an Army despatch. Thousands of crosses were awarded in both world wars and this decoration is not very highly regarded.

Five years after Napoleon instituted the *Légion d'Honneur*, Tsar Alexander I of Russia founded the Cross of St. George for award to NCOs and men. This cross carried a number of privileges: promotion to the next highest rank, exemption from corporal punishment for the rest of military service, and exemption from taxes after returning to civilian life! Holders of the cross were also awarded a pension, introduced in 1913. Vast numbers of these crosses were awarded. No fewer than 41,722 were given in the Napoleonic Wars, over 46,000 in the Russo-Turkish War of 1877 and 87,000 in the Russo-Japanese War of 1904. The exact number awarded during the First World War is not known but it is thought to have been well over 200,000. During the Crimean War Tsar Alexander II divided this award into four classes, made of gold or silver and with or without a bow in the ribbon. Many of the crosses given in the First World War were, in fact, made of bronze or white metal, owing to a shortage of precious metals. There was also a non-Christian version of the St. George Cross, for award to Moslem soldiers of the Tsar, which had the imperial eagle instead of St. George and the Dragon.

The Medal for Bravery was instituted in 1878 for NCOs and men of the armed services. It could also be awarded to women for heroic deeds and after 1910 was extended to policemen and civilians for bravery against bandits and rioters. In 1913 its name was changed to the St. George Medal. During the First World War over a million of these medals were awarded.

After the Revolution the Order of the Red Banner, instituted in 1924, became the chief Russian gallantry award. Thousands of these medals, bearing the red banner and the Russian slogan meaning 'Proletariat of all Lands, Unite', were awarded for service during the Revolution and the Civil War of 1919–23, and vast numbers were conferred during the Second World War. It has been awarded on several occasions since then, including the three officers who shot down the American U-2 spy plane in 1960.

The main Russian decoration is the gold star of Hero of the Soviet Union, instituted in 1934 for outstanding services to the country as well as conspicuous gallantry in action. During the Second World War 11,066 stars were awarded for bravery in action. Heroes of the Soviet Union who receive a second award get not only a second gold star but automatically receive the Order of Lenin. In addition a bust of the recipient is erected in a place of honour in his home town. Recipients of a third award get a second Order of Lenin and a bronze bust of themselves, with an appropriate inscription, is placed in the Palace of the Soviets at the Kremlin. Among the postwar recipients of this coveted decoration was Yuri Gagarin, the first man in space.

The Soviet Union instituted several other decorations immediately before and during the Second World War and many of these, such as the Order of Glory (1943) and the Nakhimov order and medal (1944) are given for bravery in the face of the enemy.

The premier German award for bravery was the *Ordre Pour le Mérite* (order for merit). The award was instituted as the Order of Generosity by Prince Frederick of Prussia (later King Frederick I) in 1667 and received its curious French title in 1740 from the fact that Frederick II the Great preferred the French language to his own. The decoration, an eight-pointed cross worn from a ribbon round the neck, is popularly known as the Blue Max on account of the blue enamel covering

top left The neck badge of the Order of
Leopold I. Belgium
below left The breast star of the Military
Order of Savoy which is Italy's highest
gallantry award
right The insignia of the Order of the
Rising Sun. This Japanese order was
founded in 1876

top left The Grand Cross of the *Légion d'Honneur* which is France's oldest gallantry award
below left the 4th Class neck badge of the *Légion d'Honneur*
right The insignia of the Order of the Redeemer which is one of the Greek chivalric orders

The highest honour of the USSR is the Order of Lenin. Lenin is regarded as the founder of the revolution and venerated almost as a saint

below, top row, left to right
The *Legion d'Honneur* was founded by Napoleon in 1802 and was the first French gallantry award. It has a red ribbon
The obverse and reverse of the French *Médaille Militaire* which was established in 1852 and is an equivalent to the Victoria Cross. The ribbon is yellow edged with green

bottom row, left to right
The obverse and reverse of the French *Croix de Guerre* which was established in 1915. The ribbon is light blue with red stripes
The Blue Max or *Ordre Pour Le Mérite* has not been awarded since 1918. It was the premier German award for bravery. It has a black ribbon edged with grey
The Hanza Cross of Lubeck was awarded in 1915. It has enamelled red arms and a halved red and white ribbon

the arms of the cross. Originally this order was given for civil or military distinction but in 1810, during the Napoleonic Wars, it was made an exclusively military award for gallantry. The *Pour le Mérite* was awarded in the Franco-Prussian War of 1870 and the First World War as the highest decoration, but it was discontinued after the collapse of the German Empire in 1918.

The best known of all German decorations is the Iron Cross. Originally it was instituted as a Prussian decoration by King Frederick William III in 1813, and was awarded for gallantry during the closing campaigns of the Napoleonic Wars. It had two classes which were similar in appearance except that the second class was worn from a ribbon pinned to the chest while the first class was pinned directly on to the uniform and worn like the breast star of an order, without a ribbon. There was also a Grand Cross which was awarded only nineteen times between 1813 and 1918, and a Grand Cross on a radiant star, awarded only twice —to Blucher after the Battle of Waterloo and to Field Marshal von Hindenburg in 1918. The Iron Cross was revived in 1870 and awarded during the Franco-Prussian War. It re-appeared during the

Adolf Hitler making a speech at a Nazi rally

First World War. The crosses may be found with the dates 1813, 1870 or 1914 inscribed on the lower limb. Vast numbers of Iron Crosses were awarded. Altogether there were 219,300 of the first class, and 5,500,000 of the second class, awarded between 1813 and 1918. Hitler revived the Iron Cross after the outbreak of the Second World War. The cross had the swastika in the centre and the date 1939 on the lower limb. Again, vast numbers of the cross were awarded, so that virtually every officer and enlisted man of the German armed forces received it in one form or another.

Hitler divided the Iron Cross into several classes and added some new ones. As well as the first and second class there was the Knight's Cross and this in turn could be awarded with oak leaves, swords and diamonds. Even higher was the Knight's Cross with Golden Oak Leaves and Diamonds and, highest of all, the Grand Cross, only one of which was awarded—to Reichsmarschall Goering after the surrender of France in 1940. As if such a thing should have been necessary, Hitler also instituted the War Merit Cross, as an inferior award to the Iron Cross, and this may be found in silver or bronze, with or without crossed swords depending on the class of the award. At the other end of the scale, however, Hitler instituted the German Cross (*Deutsches Kreuz*) with three classes: gold with brilliants (awarded to generals), gold for bravery in the face of the enemy, and silver for 'leadership of men' not in the face of the enemy. This decoration was worn like the star of an order, pinned directly on to the tunic.

Italy likewise introduced its highest military award at the time of the Napoleonic Wars. The Military Order of Savoy, founded by the King of Sardinia in 1815, had five classes and was intended for distinguished military service or acts of exceptional bravery. Since the fall of the monarchy in 1946 it has been renamed the Order of Military Merit of Italy. The Medal for Military Valour (*Medaglio al Valore Militare*) was introduced in 1833. The gold medal was rarely bestowed and was the Italian equivalent of the Victoria Cross. The silver and bronze versions, however, are very much more common and were given out almost as if they were campaign medals. During the First World War a series of war crosses, similar to the French *Croix de Guerre*, was instituted. Broadly speaking the war crosses rank below the medals for military valour, though in most other countries the cross of an award would rank higher than the medal.

right The Distinguished Service Cross of the Ducal Saxon-Ernestine Household Order of the Dukedoms of Saxony. It has a pink ribbon with black and yellow stripes
An Iron Cross First Class awarded in 1939. It was worn on the left breast without a ribbon

The story of the Purple Heart, America's first decoration, has already been told in a previous chapter. From 1782 until its revival in 1932 it was not awarded and for much of that period the United States had no award for bravery. In 1847 Congress instituted the Certificate of Merit which could be awarded by the President to enlisted men (privates) for distinguished conduct. In 1854 this award was extended to NCOs as well. It was not until 1905, however, that holders of the certificate were also given a medal. The certificate and medal of merit were abolished in 1918 and replaced by the Distinguished Service Medal. Since 1934 the Distinguished Service Cross has been given in circumstances where the certificate of merit would formerly have been awarded.

The Medal of Honor, America's highest award, was instituted in December 1861 for the Navy and in the following July for the Army. It may be awarded to officers or other ranks 'for bravery in action involving actual conflict with the enemy, and then only to those who distinguish themselves conspicuously by gallantry and intrepidity above and beyond the call of duty without detriment to the mission'. The decoration consists of a five-pointed bronze star worn from a ribbon round the neck. The Army version portrays Minerva, Roman goddess of war, and is surmounted by an eagle clutching thunderbolts. The naval version has a full-length portrait of Minerva repulsing Discord and is surmounted by an anchor. The blue ribbon of the medal bears thirteen stars, symbolising the original thirteen states of the Union. Although originally intended for award during the Civil War (1861–65) the Medal of Honor was retained for the minor campaigns of the nineteenth and early twentieth centuries. A new naval version, consisting of a gold cross pattee, was awarded for bravery in the First World War, but in 1942 the Navy reverted to the original design. Like the Victoria Cross, the Medal of Honor carries with it a small pension of ten dollars a month, irrespective of the rank or personal circumstance of the recipient.

In 1918, at the end of the First World War, the United States introduced several new awards. The Distinguished Service Cross was confined to the Army, but could be awarded to officers or other ranks. Its naval equivalent was the Navy Cross. The Distinguished Service Medal, both Army and Navy versions, was introduced at the

The embarkation of the 9th Army Corps at Aquia Creek landing in 1863 during the American Civil War

same time and could be awarded for exceptionally meritorious service in the field of action or 'at any other post of duty'. It thus served as the American equivalent of the British DSO. Curiously enough, between 1919 and 1942 the Navy Cross ranked below the Naval DSM; since 1942, however, the order of precedence has been reversed. In 1921 the Brevet Medal was introduced for officers of the Marine Corps who had received brevet commissions for bravery in the field. In 1926 a Distinguished Flying Cross and the Soldier's Medal were introduced respectively for heroism in the air and bravery not in the face of the enemy.

During the First World War a small silver star, worn on the ribbon of the Victory Medal, was given either for a mention in despatches or for a wound received in action. This caused a certain amount of confusion and in 1932 the original silver star was replaced by two distinctive medals. The first of these was the Purple Heart, revived in honour of the bicentenary of the birth of George Washington, and given to all those who had received wounds in the First World War or any other campaign. This medal was extended during the Second World War to all personnel who received a wound or injury (including frostbite) while on active service. Military hospitals kept a large stock of Purple Hearts in hand so that casualties could receive their medals immediately on reception. The Purple Heart is heart-shaped, of purple enamel, and portrays George Washington, surmounted by the Washington family coat of arms. The ribbon is purple with white edges. The award for a mention in despatches was recognised by the Silver Star—a bronze five-pointed star with a tiny silver star mounted in the centre.

After the United States entered the Second World War two further decorations were introduced. The Legion of Merit, perhaps modelled on Napoleon's *Légion d'Honneur*, consists of a five-rayed cross with double points, enamelled with red edges. In the centre is a blue plaque bearing the thirteen stars of the original United States. The Legion of Merit takes precedence below the Distinguished Service Medal and the Silver Star. Even lower is the Bronze Star, instituted in 1944 in recognition of service which was beyond the ordinary but not sufficient to merit the Silver Star or Legion of Merit. The Navy and Marine Corps Medal was intended as the naval equivalent of the Soldier's Medal. The last of the American military awards introduced in the Second World War was the Air Medal, a sixteen-pointed bronze star awarded automatically for shooting down an

The Legion of Merit of the United States was established during World War II. It has a white-edged maroon ribbon

enemy aircraft. It could also be awarded for distinguished service in the air while not in the presence of the enemy and in this sense is the American equivalent of the British Air Force Cross.

It should be noted that American medals and crosses are awarded irrespective of the rank of the recipient, whereas many British and European awards are limited to commissioned officers or other ranks.

Most countries now have decorations for distinguished military service or acts of bravery in time of war. Space does not permit the mention of these in detail, but among the more interesting may be cited the Czechoslovak Military Order of the White Lion for Victory (1945) and the Medal for Valour (1940), the Greek Medal of Military Merit, originally an unofficial medal instituted by Eleftherios Venizelos in 1917 when he rebelled against the Greek government but subsequently given official recognition, the Jordanian Order of Military Gallantry (*Ouisam al Ikdam al Askari*), the Israeli Medal for Heroism (*Ot Ha-Gvura*), the Japanese Order of the Golden Kite, instituted in 1891 with seven classes, the Dutch Bronze Lion (*Bronzen Leeuw*), the Norwegian War Cross, the Polish Order of Military Virtue (*Virtuti Militari*) and the Yugoslav Order of National Hero.

Several Commonwealth or former Commonwealth countries have now introduced their own gallantry awards. The Indian equivalent of the VC is known as *Param Vir Chakra*; lesser awards are the *Maha Vir Chakra* and the *Vir Chakra*. All three were established in 1950. Burma's decorations include several named in memory of Aung San, the Burmese national hero. South Africa's highest awards are the Castle of Good Hope and the Van Riebeeck Decorations, the latter being named after Jan van Riebeeck who colonised the Cape in 1652.

Many British and most foreign decorations are issued unnamed and therefore lack the personal appeal of campaign medals unless they form part of a medal group and the award can be verified. In many cases replicas have been made by jewellers (particularly in Europe) for sale to holders of decorations as duplicates, but inevitably many of these have come into the hands of collectors and are often difficult to tell from the originals. Furthermore, such is the popularity of Nazi medals and decorations that many of those now on the market are imitations. Even the humble Iron Cross, for long despised as the commonest of gallantry awards, has been forged. Such forgeries are difficult to detect and it is advisable therefore to buy only from reputable dealers.

The Castle of Good Hope is one of South Africa's highest awards. It has a green neck-ribbon

The Star of South Africa is awarded for meritorious service. It has an orange ribbon with three green stripes

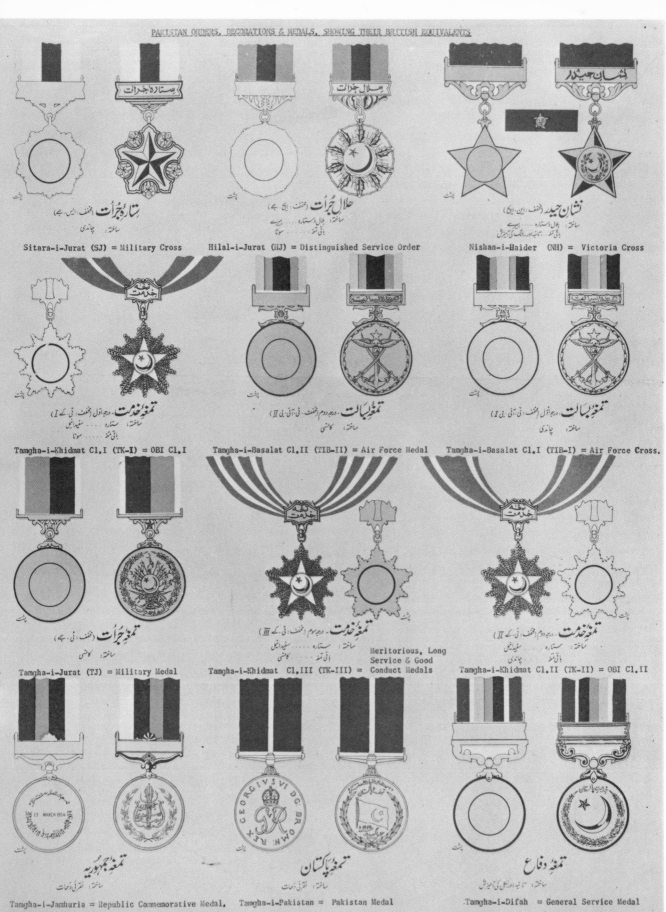

PAKISTAN ORDERS, DECORATIONS & MEDALS, SHOWING THEIR BRITISH EQUIVALENTS

Sitara-i-Jurat (SJ) = Military Cross   Hilal-i-Jurat (HJ) = Distinguished Service Order   Nishan-i-Haider (NH) = Victoria Cross

Tamgha-i-Khidmat Cl.I (TK-I) = OBI Cl.I   Tamgha-i-Basalat Cl.II (TIB-II) = Air Force Medal   Tamgha-i-Basalat Cl.I (TIB-I) = Air Force Cross.

Tamgha-i-Jurat (TJ) = Military Medal   Tamgha-i-Khidmat Cl.III (TK-III) = Meritorious, Long Service & Good Conduct Medals   Tamgha-i-Khidmat Cl.II (TK-II) = OBI Cl.II

Tamgha-i-Jamhuria = Republic Commemorative Medal.   Tamgha-i-Pakistan = Pakistan Medal   Tamgha-i-Difah = General Service Medal

5 OTHER MILITARY MEDALS

Previous chapters have dealt with medals for service in wars and campaigns or decorations for bravery in the field. Another important category consists of medals which are given for long service, good conduct, efficiency or special service. As a rule these medals are worn on the chest after gallantry awards and campaign medals, and for this reason as much as any other they tend to be neglected and despised by collectors. Perhaps it is felt that medals which are not actually connected with war service are somehow inferior. Yet many war medals were granted to personnel who never heard a shot fired in anger and who were never anywhere near the scene of fighting. Conversely a long service and good conduct medal may represent twenty or more years of 'undetected crime' and may therefore have been quite hard won by comparison. These miscellaneous medals are an interesting group in themselves and as they are often named to the recipient they frequently possess far more personal interest than many gallantry awards.

William IV instituted the first British Long Service and Good Conduct Medal in 1830, the year of his accession

previous page Sir Ernest and Lady Shackleton on board the *Endurance* before she sailed for the Antarctic in 1914

Long Service Awards

A medal for long service and good conduct was instituted by King William IV in 1830 and was awarded to soldiers of the British Army who had served for twenty-one years in the infantry or twenty in the cavalry. The LSGC, as it is usually abbreviated, was limited to warrant officers, non-commissioned officers and 'men of irreproachable character'. The earliest version of the medal featured a trophy of weapons on the obverse, and the inscription 'For long service and good conduct' on the reverse. A plain crimson ribbon was used. King Edward VII had the obverse altered and his profile substituted, and since then the portrait of the reigning sovereign has been shown. The ribbon was given white edges during the First World War to prevent it being confused with the ribbon of the Victoria Cross. It is now awarded to other ranks after the completion of eighteen years exemplary service. As a rule war service counts double, as did service in the Sudan and West Africa, on account of the unpleasant climate.

At one time each of the dominions and the more important colonies had their own distinctive LSGC medals. They followed the same design and all had a crimson ribbon, distinguished by a central stripe of another colour: dark green (Australia), light blue (New South Wales and Queensland), pink (Tasmania), orange (Cape of Good Hope), white (Canada), green (New Zealand). These and other distinctive ribbons were superseded by a crimson ribbon with a central narrow stripe of blue flanked by two narrow stripes of white. This medal was known as the Permanent Overseas Forces Long Service and Good Conduct Medal. This, in turn, has now been superseded by the medal with white edges to the crimson ribbon. A bar attached to the mounting of the ribbon indicates whether the recipient was serving in the British Regular Army or in one of the Dominion Permanent Forces. The sole exception to this was the version awarded to members of the Bechuanaland Protectorate Police, which was inscribed BECHUANALAND.

Several of the Commonwealth countries have also produced their own medals. New Zealand had a Long and Efficient Service Medal, for sixteen years' consecutive service, and a Territorial Service Medal, for twelve years' service in the Territorial Force. These medals have long been obsolete. The latter was superseded by the Efficiency Decoration and the Efficiency Medal (for officers and other ranks respectively) after compulsory military service was abolished in 1936. Since the Second World War, however, New Zealand has used the British LSGC medal. Canada instituted the Canadian Forces Decoration in 1950 and awarded it to all ranks of the regular and reserve forces who completed twelve years' service under certain conditions. This decoration, known as the CD, replaced all the long service, good conduct and efficiency medals previously awarded. South Africa likewise introduced its own distinctive service medals after the Second World War. The John Chard Medal is awarded for twelve years' service in the armed forces. Recipients of this medal may then go on to win the John Chard Decoration which is awarded to all ranks for a minimum of eight years' active service and twelve years' in the reserves. Both the medal and the decoration depict a view of Rorke's Drift where Lieutenant John Chard of the Royal Engineers won his Victoria Cross in 1879 during the Zulu War. The Union Medal is awarded to servicemen after completing eighteen years' exemplary service.

Similar medals were awarded to European and native NCOs and men in the Indian Army. These medals became obsolete when India attained independence and they have now been replaced by their republican equivalents. Similar medals have also been introduced in Pakistan, Ghana and Malaysia.

The first naval LSGC medal appeared in 1831 and had a dark blue ribbon. Later a navy blue ribbon with white edges was substituted. The naval medal was awarded to petty officers and ratings for fifteen years exemplary service. A similar medal, with narrow crimson stripes towards either edge of its ribbon, was awarded to members of the Royal Fleet Reserve.

Other British awards which may be encountered include the Meritorious Service Medal which, as has been mentioned in the previous chapter, was originally intended as a gallantry award, but is now granted to holders of the LSGC for additional long and exemplary service. At one time it was possible to win a bar to the MSM for further terms of service or exceptional devotion to duty, but this function was replaced in 1928 and the British Empire Medal awarded instead. Although originally an Army award the MSM was extended in 1919 to the Navy and the Royal Marines. A Royal Air Force MSM existed for a brief period after the First World War, but was replaced by the British Empire Medal in 1928. Since then the RAF version of the LSGC, featuring an eagle and the British

The John Chard Medal is awarded by South Africa for twelve years service in the forces. It has a red ribbon with blue edges and white stripes

above, left
The reverse of the Royal Naval Volunteer Reserve Long Service and Good Conduct Medal. It has a blue, red and green ribbon
right The British War Medal in Bronze was awarded mostly to the half million Chinese who served in France during World War I

The Territorial Decoration was instituted in 1908. It has a dark green ribbon with a central yellow stripe

crown, has been the only RAF award for long service.

Long service awards for the volunteer forces date back to 1892 when the Volunteer Officers' Decoration was instituted for officers who had served for twenty years. A similar decoration was established in 1894 for the volunteer forces in India but service in that case was reduced to eighteen years. The decoration consisted of a silver wreath with bands of gold and the royal cypher in gold in the centre. There was also a silver Volunteer Long Service Medal for other ranks. Both decoration and medal were abolished in 1908 and superseded by the Efficiency Decoration and the Efficiency Medal when the Territorial Force was founded. In addition there were, at one time, similar decorations and medals for the Colonial Auxiliary Forces, the Militia, the Imperial Yeomanry and the Army Emergency Reserve. The Royal Naval Reserve and the Royal Naval Volunteer Reserve also have their distinctive service medals. In addition there are distinctive long service medals for the Wireless Auxiliary Reserve and the Auxiliary Sick Berth Reserve of the Royal Navy. In 1942 the Air Efficiency Award was established for long service in the Auxiliary and Volunteer Air Forces, the minimum being ten years. The Cadet Forces Medal was instituted in 1950 for award to officers and instructors who had served with cadet units for twelve years. The medal features the torch of learning on the reverse. Long service in the Special Constabulary and the Royal Observer Corps is also recognised by the award of appropriate medals for nine and twelve years respectively.

The armed forces of the United States also have a wide variety of good conduct and long service medals. Separate medals are awarded by the Army, Navy, Marine Corps, Coast Guard and the reserve forces. The Navy Good Conduct Medal was authorised as long ago as 1869 but it was not until June 1941 that the Army followed suit. Service stars and medals were awarded by both Belgium and France for service in their respective colonies. Many of the old German states had similar medals for long service and these can usually be recognised by the inclusion of the word DIENST (service) in their inscriptions. Medals inscribed *'Voor Langdurige Dienst'* are Dutch and were granted to officers, NCOs and men for long service. The Army medal was instituted in 1825 and the naval medal twenty years later. These medals were awarded in gold, silver or bronze, depending on the length of service.

Captain Scott led several expeditions to the Antarctic but tragically died during the last. *left* Sir Vivian Fuchs who led the big Transantarctic Expedition in 1956

Polar Medals

Service in the Arctic or Antarctic is recognised by the award of medals which were first authorised as long ago as 1857. The first Arctic Medal was retrospective, and was given to officers and men who had taken part in various expeditions between 1818 and 1855. The silver medal was octagonal in shape, portrayed Queen Victoria on the obverse and depicted a ship and icebergs with a sledging party in the foreground. A plain white ribbon was worn with this medal. A second medal, circular in shape, was instituted in 1876 and awarded to the crews of ships which took part in the expedition of 1875–76.

King Edward VII instituted the Polar Medal in 1904 for Captain Scott's National Antarctic Expedition of 1901–4. Like the first of these medals the Polar Medal was octagonal. The reverse showed Scott's ship *Discovery*, with a sledging party in the foreground. The crew of the *Discovery* received the medal in silver with the clasp 'Antarctic 1901–1904'. Crews of the relief ships *Morning* and *Terra Nova* received the medal in bronze without clasp. Three years later the medal was awarded for Shackleton's Antarctic Ex-

Roald Amundsen was awarded a gold medal by the Norwegian government in recognition of his expeditions which explored both the Arctic and Antarctic

pedition and in 1913 it was awarded to the survivors of Scott's last expedition, the effigy on this medal being that of King George V. Subsequently the Polar Medal was awarded to the Mawson expedition (1912–14), Shackleton's Imperial Trans-Antarctic Expedition (1914–16) and for various expeditions between 1929 and 1937. A new version of the Polar Medal, with the profile of King George VI, appeared in 1943 with the clasp 'Arctic 1940–42' and was awarded to the crew of the Royal Canadian Mounted Police schooner *St. Roche* for exploring the North-west Arctic regions of Canada. Subsequently a clasp for 'Arctic 1944' was awarded to personnel of the same ship for further research work. The bronze medals are no longer issued, but since 1953 there have been silver medals with the effigy of Queen Elizabeth and clasps inscribed 'Arctic' or 'Antarctic', with the appropriate dates of various polar expeditions up to the present time. In many cases the award of Polar Medals and clasps has been confined to a handful of men. It has been estimated that awards for service in the polar regions since the beginning of this century amount to fewer than a thousand altogether and when it is realised that over 90 different bars have been authorised, it will be seen that the Polar Medal is, in fact, an extremely rare item. The commonest award is the medal with clasp 'Antarctic 1910–13' for Scott's last expedition, 50 medals and 63 clasps being awarded. In many cases in recent years only one or two clasps of a particular date have been awarded. Although the bronze medal was intended as a lesser award it is by far the scarcer of the two awards. Additional clasps are correspondingly scarce, the record being the silver medal with four clasps won by Commander Frank Wild, who commanded the *Quest* on Shackleton's last voyage in 1921–22.

Polar medals have been awarded by other countries. The best known of these are the medals issued by the United States. Congress authorised a medal in 1944 to be given to members of the expedition led by Admiral Peary to the North Pole in 1908–9. Both of the Byrd Antarctic Expeditions (1928–30 and 1933–35) were honoured by the award of special medals. Medals were struck in gold, silver or bronze for the first expedition, by authority of Congress in May 1930 and portrayed Admiral Byrd on the obverse. A silver medal was authorised in 1936 for presentation to personnel of the second expedition and again Admiral Byrd's portrait was used. In 1945 Congress sanctioned a medal for the Antarctic expedition of 1939–41 and more recent expeditions have been similarly honoured. Norway awarded a gold South Pole medal to members of Roald Amundsen's expedition of 1910–11. The earliest of all polar medals was the bronze medal instituted in 1821 by Tsar Alexander I and awarded to the officers and men of the ships *Vostok* and *Mirny* who explored the Arctic seas under the command of Admiral Bellingshausen in 1819–21. The obverse portrayed the Tsar while the rather plain reverse bore the names of the ships and the date. This medal was worn with the ribbon of the Order of St. Anne. Oddly enough, though Russia has taken an active part in the exploration of both polar regions no special medals have been produced for this purpose since 1821.

Commemorative Medals

The vast majority of commemorative medals are unofficial in character and since they are a specialised branch of the subject are treated separately in Chapter 8. But quite a number of miscellaneous medals which have been awarded to military personnel are also commemorative in nature. As has already been mentioned, Russia has long favoured this kind of medal, issuing it to service personnel to mark important military anniversaries. In Tsarist times sailors and soldiers were also awarded medals to celebrate the coronation of the Tsar or in his memory after his death.

Coronation medals in England date back to the accession of the boy-king Edward VI. These medals were cast in gold or silver and were presented to courtiers as a memento of the occasion. No coronation medals were produced for either Mary or Elizabeth, but medals were struck by the Royal Mint to mark the accession of King James I in 1603 and for distribution among the crowds who celebrated his coronation. The latter bore the curious title 'Caesar Augustus of Britain and Heir to the Caesars'. Since that time medals have been struck regularly to mark each coronation. Many of the official medals struck in the eighteenth and nineteenth centuries were intended as presentation pieces and were not meant to be worn. However, for the coronation of King Edward VII in 1902 a silver medal was struck and mounted with a suspender and ribbon of blue with a thin white stripe and scarlet edges. This medal was given to notable personages attending the coronation, but subsequently coronation medals came to be regarded as an award for services rendered in connection with the coronation ceremony. It has been

The boy king Edward VI was the first English Monarch to have coronation medals struck in his honour

given to troops lining the route of the coronation procession, as well as to officials from the Earl Marshal of England downwards. In more recent times the coronation medal has even been given to people who were not present at the coronation but who performed a notable public service in the coronation year. Medals of this kind were awarded for the coronations of George V (1911), George VI (1937) and Queen Elizabeth (1953). In addition a special medal was awarded in 1935 to celebrate the Silver Jubilee of King George V.

Coronation medals were also struck by Japan, for the Emperor Hirohito in 1928, by the Netherlands, for Queen Wilhelmina in 1898 and Queen Juliana in 1948, by Norway for King Haakon in 1906 and King Olav in 1958. Though Sweden has not issued coronation medals it has made up for this in the wide range of other royal events for which medals have been awarded. Among the royal occasions on which medals have been struck are King Oscar's Jubilee (1897), the 70th and 90th birthdays of King Gustav V (1928 and 1948), King Oscar's Golden Wedding, (1907) and Crown Prince Gustav's Silver Wedding (1906). A 70th birthday medal was issued after the Second World War and awarded to all personnel who served in the armed forces in 1942, the actual year of King Haakon's birthday. At that time Norway was under Nazi occupation and the King was in exile in Britain. A medal with a very colourful ribbon was awarded by the Netherlands in 1937 to celebrate the wedding of Princess Juliana and Prince Bernhard.

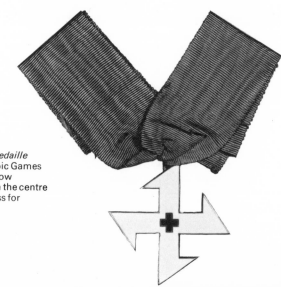

above The Nazi Olympia *Erinnerungsmedaille* which commemorated the 1936 Olympic Games held in Berlin. It has a black-edged yellow ribbon with five narrow white stripes in the centre *right* The Queen Marie of Romania Cross for Nursing. It has an orange ribbon

6 ORDERS OF CHIVALRY

The most colourful and romantic of all medals and decorations are those connected with the orders of chivalry. Many of them have their origins in the Middle Ages, when knights in armour formed the elite fighting force in every European country. This was the period when knights jousted in tournaments as a pastime, between going off to the Holy Land on the wars of Christendom known as the Crusades. This was the era of such popular heroes as Richard the Lionheart, William the Lion, the Black Prince, Baudouin of Constantinople, Robert of Jerusalem and John the Blind King of Bohemia. Their exploits have passed into the folklore of Europe, together with the legends of Roland and his Paladins or King Arthur and the Knights of the Round Table.

previous page This picture of Kaiser Wilhelm II shows him wearing various German orders that were abolished after the Armistice in 1918

Edward III was very interested in the legends of King Arthur and the knights of the Round Table. He tried to get his court to imitate Camelot

From the idea of a select band of knights, pledged to the support of a king or an ideal (usually religious), sprang the orders of knighthood. Many of these existed in the Middle Ages but most of them died out as feudalism went into decline. In some cases they survived; in others they disappeared for centuries, only to be resurrected at a later date. In their original form these orders of chivalry were just as highly coveted, but the insignia was usually simple or quite non-existent. The complicated system of insignia which now surrounds these orders is fairly modern, dating from the sixteenth century or later. Nowadays most orders also exist in several classes, with the insignia becoming increasingly elaborate with each higher class.

Britain's senior order of knighthood is the Garter, and though it consists of one class only it provides a good example of the pomp and ceremony which often surrounds these awards. The order was founded by King Edward III in 1348 and is said to derive its name from the fact that the king was attending a dance one day, when a lady's garter slipped from her leg and fell to the floor. To save her the embarrassment of retrieving her garter—and thus letting everyone know that it was hers—the king himself picked it up and tied it round his own leg. Lest anyone should doubt that it was his garter he said, in court French, 'Let evil be to him who evil thinks'. From this curious incident came the idea of a very exclusive order of knighthood, consisting of the king and 26 knights. The chief emblem of this order is the Garter, of dark blue velvet trimmed with gold thread and embroidered with the French words *Honi soit qui mal y pense*, which King Edward used on the famous occasion. The Queen, as present sovereign, wears the Garter on her left arm, whereas the knights wear it on the left leg below the knee.

The insignia of the Garter also includes a mantle of blue velvet lined with taffeta, with the star of the order embroidered on the left breast, a hood of crimson velvet, a surcoat of crimson velvet, lined with white taffeta, a hat of black velvet, lined with white taffeta, with a plume of white ostrich and black heron feathers fastened by a band of diamonds, a collar of gold composed of buckled garters and lovers' knots with red roses, the George (an enamelled figure of St. George fighting the dragon) suspended from the collar, the lesser George or badge, worn from a broad blue sash passing over the left shoulder to the right hip, and the star, a silver eight-pointed decoration

bearing the red cross of St. George surrounded by the garter and motto.

The full insignia is only worn on special occasions; usually the lesser George and the breast star are worn on their own. On the death of the knight the insignia must be returned to the Central Chancery of Knighthood, and therefore few examples of the Garter ever come on to the market. Those that do are usually examples from the seventeenth and eighteenth centuries when regulations regarding the return of insignia were not so strict. Knights of the Garter, as well as holders of other orders, frequently have replicas of breast stars made for use on different uniforms and it is often difficult to tell these replicas from the originals since in many cases the replicas were made by the court jewellers responsible for making the originals. In addition many jewellers in such European capitals as Vienna, Berlin and Paris have a long tradition of manufacturing the insignia of orders for sale to collectors. Like the awards and decorations mentioned in Chapter 4, these items are seldom named to the recipient and for this reason do not command the same interest or respect of collectors. Nevertheless, in cases where the insignia of orders can be definitely proved to have belonged to some famous person, the interest and value are enhanced. In any case these orders are usually very attractive examples of the jeweller's art, and they often have names and stories as colourful as their appearance.

If the Garter may be regarded as an essentially English order its two companions may be regarded as its Scottish and Irish counterparts. The Most Ancient and Most Noble Order of the Thistle, as its full title implies, can boast an even greater antiquity than the Garter, having been founded by the King of Scots in 787. At some time in the dim and distant past, however, it died out and was not revived until 1687 by King James II and took its present form in 1703. It consists of the sovereign and sixteen knights, and is therefore one of the most exclusive orders in existence. The Most Illustrious Order of St. Patrick was founded by King George III in 1783 and was limited to the sovereign, the Lord Lieutenant of Ireland and 22 knights. Both the Thistle and St. Patrick orders have impressive insignia which must be returned on the death of the recipient.

top The Most Noble Order of the Garter is one of the oldest chivalric orders and was founded in 1348 by Edward III *The illustration is ¼ actual size.*
above The Most Illustrious Order of St. Patrick was founded in 1783 by George III and became obsolete in 1922. It was the premier order of Ireland. The only surviving holder is H.R.H. The Duke of Gloucester *The illustration is ¼ actual size.*

above The Most Eminent Order of the Indian Empire was founded in 1878 by Queen Victoria as a reward for distinguished service in India. It became obsolete in 1947
below The Most Distinguished Order of St. Michael and St. George was founded in 1818 by George III. Its function was changed in 1859 to reward distinguished overseas service

Below the three premier orders of knighthood comes the Most Honourable Order of the Bath, founded in 1399. It takes its name from the ritual bathing of the would-be knights to ensure their purity before being invested with their insignia. Bear in mind that taking a bath was a very rare occurrence, even in polite circles, in medieval times. As late as the reign of Queen Elizabeth it could be said that the Queen took a bath once a month 'whether she needed it or not'. Whether the institution of this order resulted in a higher standard of hygiene at Court is not known, but eventually the Order of the Bath fell into disuse. It was revived by King George I in 1725 and consisted originally of one class only. The KB, as it was then known, was awarded to generals and admirals for distinguished war service. After the Battle of Waterloo the order was expanded into three classes—Knights Grand Cross (GCB), Knights Commander (KCB) and Companions (CB). The abbreviation KB is now used to signify Knights Bachelor, who do not receive a specific knighthood but who get a breast star bearing a cross-hilted sword and spurs, the medieval symbols of knighthood. In 1847 award of the Bath was thrown open to civilians, who now wear similar insignia but have a slightly different ribbon.

Several other British orders of knighthood may be encountered, but are all now obsolete. The Royal Guelphic Order of Hanover was founded by the Prince Regent in 1815 but went out of use after the death of William IV in 1837, when Hanover ceased to be linked to Britain. The eight-pointed star featured the white horse of Hanover. This order was divided into two classes (civil and military) each of which had three classes—knight grand cross, knight commander and knight—and was frequently awarded to Service chiefs and prominent civil servants. Distinguished military or civil service in India was rewarded by either the Most Eminent Order of the Indian Empire (founded in 1878) or the Most Exalted Order of the Star of India (instituted in 1861). Both orders became obsolete in 1947 when India and Pakistan became independent.

Conversely one order of knighthood, originally founded for award to non-British subjects, has now been adopted for British subjects, though usually for service abroad. The Most Distinguished Order of St. Michael and St. George was founded by King George III in 1818 to reward citizens of the Ionian Islands which came under British rule during the Napoleonic Wars. The islands were given to Greece in 1859 but the order, instead of becoming obsolete, was then awarded to British subjects for distinguished service overseas. It is divided into three classes—Knights Grand Cross (GCMG), Knights Commander (KCMG) and Companions (CMG)—and the abbreviations gave rise to the joke that holders of this award could say respectively, 'Call me God', 'Kindly call me God' and 'God calls me God.'

The most recent, and also the commonest, British order of knighthood is the Most Excellent Order of the British Empire, instituted by King George V in June 1917. It is by far the most complicated of the British orders, with two divisions (military and civil) each consisting of five classes open to both men and women. The number of possible different variations in the insignia, according to the division, class or sex of the recipient is quite large. Ladies in the two upper classes of the order receive the title of Dame. In addition to the ranks of Knights Grand Cross, Knights Commanders, Commanders, Officers and Members are the holders of the British Empire Medal, which has already been dealt with in Chapter 4.

Normally orders of chivalry, or their higher classes at least, also carry a distinctive title— 'Sir' or 'Dame'. Wives of knights automatically receive the title of 'Lady', but husbands of Dames have to remain plain Mister—a case of discrimination which ought to be taken up by Men's Lib! There are, however, two other orders which, though very exclusive, do not carry any distinctive title. The Order of Merit was founded by King Edward VII in 1902 and is awarded for exceptional services to the country. The enamelled convex cross pattee is worn from a ribbon round the neck. The Order of the Companions of Honour was instituted in June 1917 and consists of the sovereign and no more than fifty Companions. The oval badge, showing a knight in armour, is worn round the neck. Companions use the letters CH after their names but do not receive any title.

At one time the King had the right to bestow honours and knighthoods, but this has long been taken over by Parliament and the Ministers of the Crown. The sovereign still has one order to bestow, and that is the Royal Victorian Order, given for personal services to the Royal Family. It has five classes, ranging from the Knight Grand Cross (GCVO) to the Members of the Fifth Class (MVO), and below that there is the Royal Victorian Medal, in silver-gilt, silver or bronze, awarded for lesser services.

Of the foreign orders of knighthood now extant,

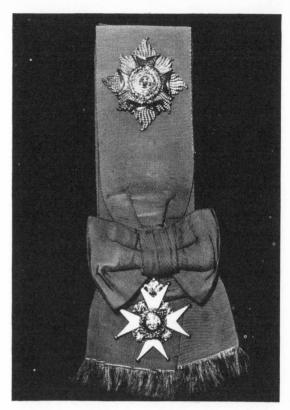

The Most Honourable Order of the Bath was revived in 1725 by George I and was enlarged in 1815 to include two divisions of civilians and military *The illustration is ¼ actual size.*

A Knight's Cross of the Order of the British Empire. The ribbon is purple with a central scarlet stripe indicating the Military division

those of Portugal are probably the oldest. The Military Order of St. Benedict of Aviz was introduced to Portugal from Spain in 1162 as a religious military order, but it was taken over as a secular order by Queen Maria in 1789 for military or naval merit. The Order of St. James of the Sword likewise came from Spain, in 1177, and was also secularised in 1789. In 1862 it was designated as an order of merit for services in science, literature or art. The Military Order of Christ was instituted in 1317 in conjunction with Pope John XXII, but became an exclusively Portuguese order in 1522. Like its predecessors it was secularised in 1789. The Military Order of the Tower and Sword was founded by Alfonso V in 1459 and revived in 1808 by John, Prince Regent of Portugal, to commemorate his safe arrival in Brazil, after Napoleon's armies drove him out of Portugal. It was reorganised in 1832 as an order of civil and military merit.

Spain possesses one of the most famous of all medieval orders—the Golden Fleece. The emblem of this order is a sheepskin of gold, suspended round the recipient's neck. The exact origin of this order is not known. It may have derived from the Greek myth of Jason and the Argonauts who went to Colchis to get the fabled Golden Fleece. In fact the order was founded by Philip the Good, Duke of Burgundy, in January 1430 to celebrate his marriage with Isabella of Portugal at Bruges in what is now Belgium. It is thought that the Duke took the fleece as his emblem on account of the fact that his fortune was made largely from the Flemish wool trade. The order consisted of 24 knights only. The Golden Fleece became the premier Austrian order of knighthood following the marriage of Mary of Burgundy with Maximilian of Austria in 1477. It came to Spain in 1504 on the accession of Philip, son of Mary and Maximilian, to the throne of Castile. The Golden Fleece, like the Garter, was traditionally aristocratic, and was conferred only on members of the Royal Family, foreign heads of state and members of the nobility. The other Spanish orders still in use are more modern in origin. The orders of Charles III (1771), St. Ferdinand (1811), St. Hermengilde (1814) and Maria Cristina (1890) all have several classes, both military and civil. The Royal American Order of Isabella the Catholic was founded in 1815 in memory of Isabella of Castile whose encouragement of Christopher Columbus has given her a special place in American history. This order was conferred for services in the defence of the Spanish colonies in America at a time when most

The Spanish Order of Alphonso XII. This is a Grand Cross set with sash badge and breast star

The Order of the Golden Fleece has been the premier order of both Austria (in the fifteenth century) and Spain. This one was conferred upon the Duke of Wellington after the Peninsular Campaigns

The Duke of Wellington was one of the most
decorated men ever. Here he is wearing the
collar of the Golden Fleece and the sash and
star of a Knight Commander of the Royal
Guelphic Order of Hanover. *below* The 1st Duke
of Marlborough wearing a contemporary
Garter Star *and right* George II wearing the
Garter Collar Chain and George

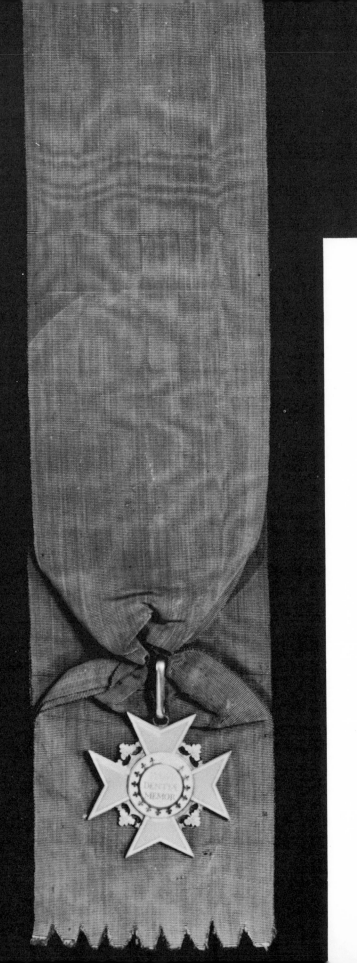

The Order of the Crown. An order of the Duchy of Saxony which was awarded to the Duke of Wellington

of these colonies were fighting their long war for independence against the motherland. Now that Spain has no colonies in America this order is bestowed for general services.

There are many other Spanish orders, mostly of comparatively recent origin. Of these the most colourful is the Yoke and Arrows (*Yugo y Flechas*) instituted by General Franco. It is said to be based on an ancient emblem signifying the arrows of Spain freeing the country from the yoke of the Moors.

The premier order of knighthood in Sweden is the Order of the Seraphim, founded either in 1280 or 1336, but reconstituted by Frederick I in 1748. Lesser orders are the Order of the Sword, founded for military service in 1522, the Order of the Pole Star, dating from 1748, the Order of Vasa, instituted in 1772 for service to industry, and the Order of Charles XIII, founded in 1811 for award to Freemasons who have attained the highest degrees. Denmark has the Order of Dannebrog, founded by Waldemar II in 1219. It was revived in 1671 and now consists of six classes, plus a seventh which receives the Dannebrog Badge of Honour, the Danish equivalent of the British Empire Medal. The highest Danish order is the quaintly named Order of the Elephant, dating from 1462. The badge and star of this order are richly studded with diamonds and have to be returned to the Danish authorities on the death of the recipient. Considerable embarrassment was caused in the 1950s when the Egyptian Government tried to auction the orders and decorations left behind by King Farouk when he fled into exile. These included the Order of the Elephant, and long and involved negotiations followed before the insignia could be returned to Copenhagen.

The Grand Cross of the Order of Fidelity, awarded to the Duke of Wellington by the Duchy of Baden

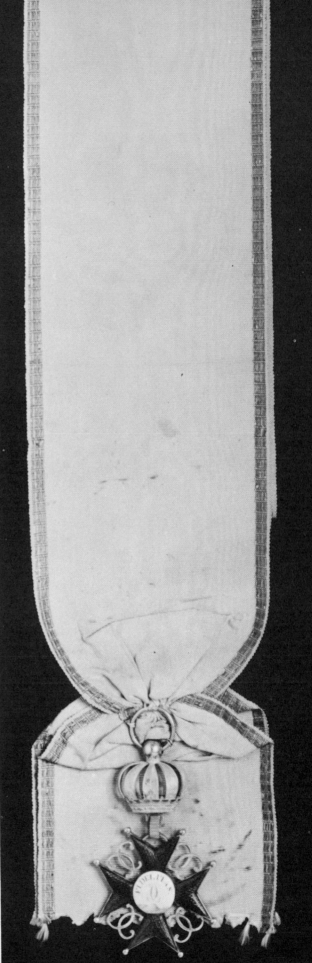

The German Empire had numerous orders of knighthood, all of which were swept away in 1918. The Nazi orders were mostly for military service and have already been referred to, but in 1937 Hitler instituted the Order of Merit of the German Eagle with five classes, ranging from the Grand Cross to the Cross of Merit Third Class. When Hitler visited Mussolini in Rome in 1937 he bestowed on the Italian dictator a special gold Grand Cross suspended from a unique multi-coloured ribbon. In 1951 the German Federal Republic instituted a new Order of Merit consisting of eight classes from Grand Cross to Merit Cross.

The highest order in Italy was the Annunziata. Founded in 1362 it was limited to fifteen knights who were entitled to the description 'cousins of the king': Like the Garter this order had magnificent insignia, the most important part of which was the Collar. The Annunziata was very rarely awarded. In 1939 King Victor Emmanuel III was forced, against his will, to confer this decoration on Von Ribbentrop, the Nazi Foreign Minister. Count Ciano, the Italian Foreign Minister and son-in-law of Mussolini, later recorded in his diary how Goering had burst into tears of rage when he saw Ribbentrop wearing the Annunziata. Goering made a terrible scene, crying bitterly that the decoration really belonged to him, since he was the only true promoter of the Italo-German Alliance. As a result, King Victor Emmanuel was forced to award a second Annunziata, to Goering, the following year as a matter of diplomacy. Goering's love of medals and decorations was a standing joke, both inside Germany and outside, although in fairness it should be pointed out that he had won the *Pour le Mérite* and other high

Reichmarshall Goering making a speech. He was the only man ever to receive the Grand Cross of the Iron Cross

above left The Order of Merit was founded in 1902 by Edward VII and is an award for exceptional service to the country. It has a blue and purple ribbon

right Neck-badge of the Military Order of St Heinrichs-Ordens of the Duchy of Saxony

German decorations as an air ace during the First World War.

Tsarist Russia had numerous orders of knighthood, all of which were distinguished by stars and insignia studded with costly jewels. The highest order was that of St. Andrew, founded by Peter the Great in 1698. Award of this order automatically entitled the recipient to all the other orders— St. Alexander Nevsky, the White Eagle, St. Anne and St. Stanislas. The White Eagle was originally a Polish order but was taken over by the Russians in 1831 after the so-called Congress Kingdom of Poland was incorporated into the Tsar's dominions. The other orders all dated from the early eighteenth century. The Order of St. Vladimir, founded in 1782, was originally a civilian order but during the Crimean War it was extended to army and naval officers as well.

All of the Tsarist orders were abolished after the 1917 Revolution. Two orders were established in the 1920s by the Grand Duke Kyrille Vladimirovich, as rightful heir to the Imperial throne. The Order of St Nicholas the Miracle Worker was founded in memory of Tsar Nicholas II. Both this order and the Order of the Compassionate Heart could be obtained by any veteran of the Tsarist forces now living in exile.

The Soviet Union has a large number of orders and those which are primarily intended as gallantry awards have already been mentioned. The premier civil order is the Order of Lenin, instituted in 1930 in memory of the founder of the Soviet state. The highest military order is the Order of Victory instituted in 1943. Among the other orders are those named in memory of past naval and military heroes—Suvorov, Ushakov, Kutuzov, Nakhimov and Bogdan Khmelnitsky, the last of which was primarily a Ukrainian award. The Tsarist Order of St. Alexander Nevsky was revived by the Communists in 1942 for distinguished military or naval service. The Soviet version of the star portrays the saint, with the hammer and the sickle emblem at the foot.

The countries of Asia borrowed European traditions of knighthood and instituted their own orders of chivalry. Japan has the orders of the Chrysanthemum (1876), the Rising Sun (1876) and the Sacred Treasure (1888). The sultanates of Malaysia and the sheikhdoms of Arabia all have colourful orders, many of which have been conferred on British officers and administrators at various times.

No account of orders of chivalry would be complete without some reference to those orders

above Various pieces of insignia of the Russian Order of St. Anne which was founded in the early eighteenth century

right The highest Russian order was the Order of St. Andrew which was founded by Peter the Great. This one was awarded to the Duke of Wellington

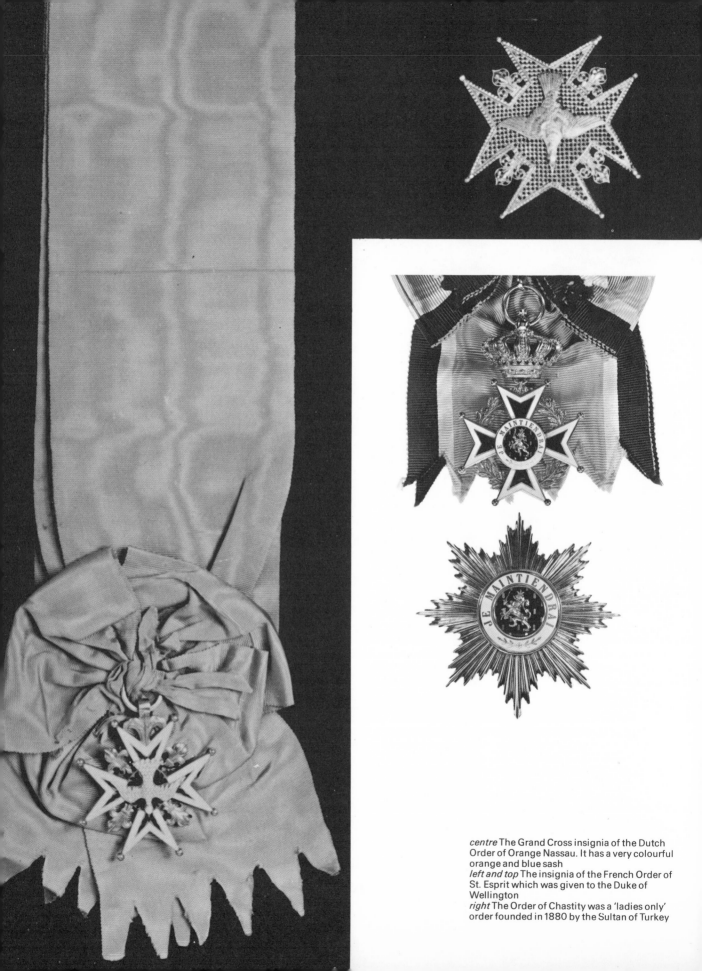

centre The Grand Cross insignia of the Dutch Order of Orange Nassau. It has a very colourful orange and blue sash
left and top The insignia of the French Order of St. Esprit which was given to the Duke of Wellington
right The Order of Chastity was a 'ladies only' order founded in 1880 by the Sultan of Turkey

which have been founded in recent years for award specifically to women. The Royal Order of Victoria and Albert was founded by Queen Victoria in 1862 and comprised the Queen and 45 ladies. The first two classes are limited to ladies of the British and other royal families, while membership of the two other classes is open to women who have performed outstanding services. King George IV established a Royal Family Order whose decoration, a miniature portrait of the ruler set in precious stones, is worn only by ladies of the Royal Family. This custom has continued with each successive sovereign down to the present day.

In Greece the Order of St. Olga and St. Sophia was confined to ladies of noble birth and existed in four classes. The Welfare Order, likewise limited to women, was awarded in five classes for outstanding social work or nursing services. The Spanish Order of Maria-Louisa was founded in 1792 by the wife of Charles IV and was awarded to ladies of the aristocracy. The Order of Chastity was founded by the Turkish Sultan in 1880 for award to ladies. On the other hand the Soviet Union has the Order of Mother Heroine, instituted in 1944 and awarded to mothers who have given birth to and brought up ten or more children. Recipients receive the title of Mother Heroine, a state pension and reduced travel concessions on public transport. Lower down the scale there is also the Order of the Glory of Motherhood, consisting of three classes, awarded to mothers of nine, eight and seven children respectively. Between its inception and 1968 over 2,250,000 Soviet housewives had received this order in one or other of its classes. A similar decoration was awarded in Nazi Germany during the Second World War.

The Grand Cross insignia of the Austria Order of Francis Joseph. The motto on both badges is *Viribus Unitus*

The Nazi Mothers' Cross of Honour in gold, silver and bronze. The gold was awarded for eight or more children, the silver for six or seven and the bronze for four or five

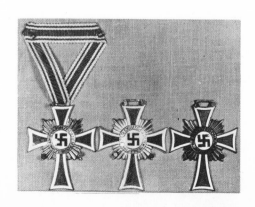

A print of Grace Darling and her father rowing to the wreck

7 CIVIL DECORATIONS

There are many miscellaneous medals and decorations which are primarily civil rather than military in character. Of course many of the awards mentioned in previous chapters either have civil divisions or were open to civilians and service personnel alike. In 1902 King Edward VII instituted the Imperial Service Order and the Imperial Service Medal as a means of rewarding

This medal was struck by General Gordon during the Siege of Khartoum and distributed to encourage morale

outstanding service in the administrative or clerical branches of the civil service. The ISO may be awarded for long service (the qualifying period for which is 25 years in Britain, 20 years in India or 16 years in unhealthy climates such as West Africa) but more often it is now awarded to people who were perhaps nominated for the MBE and failed to receive this award. The ISO is much rarer than the MBE and is now seldom awarded. The ISM, in many respects, corresponds with the BEM. Both of these awards rank after other decorations, both civil and military and are worn after campaign medals.

General George Gordon was the Governor of the Sudan when the Mahdi's rebellion broke out. He died in Khartoum when the Mahdi's troops stormed and took the city

An important class of medals and decorations is those awarded by the Grand Priory in the British Realm of the Most Venerable Order of St. John of Jerusalem—to give it its full title. The Order of St. John of Jerusalem has had a long and chequered history from its foundation in the eleventh century to give aid and hospitality to knights on their way to fight in the Holy Land. The Knights were driven out of Jerusalen and for a time held the island of Rhodes against the Turks. In 1530 they were driven out of Rhodes and moved their headquarters to Malta where they successfully repulsed the Turks in the Great Siege of 1565. They were evicted by Napoleon in 1798 and now have their headquarters in Rome. The order now has branches in most European countries, the British branch having been established in 1888. In 1926 the British Order was granted the title Venerable and re-organised into five classes, with appropriate insignia. Queen Elizabeth is the Sovereign Head of the Order and below her come the Grand Prior, the Bailiffs and Dames Grand Cross, the Knights and Dames of Justice, the Knights and Dames of Grace, the Commanders, the Officers, the Serving Brothers and the Serving Sisters. The insignia of the Order includes the distinctive eight-pointed Maltese cross. In addition there are the St. John of Jerusalem Life-Saving Medal and the Service Medal of the Order of St. John.

In 1902 King Edward VII instituted a medal for Science, Art and Music. It was discontinued four years later and it is not known how many of these medals were awarded. The King and Queen Alexandra were portrayed on the obverse while a group of figures symbolising the arts and sciences was shown on the reverse. No separate awards of this nature have been made since then, though the Order of the British Empire is now used freely for this purpose.

Most countries, however, have a wide range of civil decorations and medals for award to different sections of the community. The most prolific of these come from France. At the top of the tree there is the *Palme Universitaire* (academic palm), founded by Napoleon in 1808. It exists in two groups, *Officier de l'Instruction Publique* and *Officier d'Academie*, and both are awarded on the recommendation of the Minister of Education to those who have distinguished themselves in the fields of learning and teaching and in the arts and sciences. A higher class, of *Commandeur*, was introduced in 1945. The decoration, in gold or silver, consists of two sprays of palm leaves joined at the top and bottom. In 1883 three orders were instituted for agricultural merit, commercial merit and social merit respectively. Subsequently the French government has introduced medals and orders for almost every branch of the civil services in France and the overseas territories, as well as to private individuals in many walks of life who excel in their various professions. Among the different awards (now running to more than thirty) now in existence are the orders of Working-class Merit, Tourist Merit, the Order of National Economy, the orders of Public Health and Postal Merit. Medals are also awarded to physical education, communal workers, teachers, forestry workers, prison officers, members of musical societies, railway employees, tax officials, customs officers, nurses, gendarmes, savings bank employees and mutual help societies. In addition there are somewhat general medals for encouragement to devotion and encouragement to good.

The countries of the Communist bloc have also been prolific in awarding medals and decorations to members of the public and civil servants for loyal service. Many of these countries have an Order of Labour or Hero of Socialist Labour, which can be awarded for long service and good conduct in offices and factories. The Soviet Union has a large number of these medals, for 'valiant labour' or 'labour distinction', but even in Tsarist times there were many medals designed to reward good behaviour among the working classes and peasantry. There were medals for census officers, school-teachers, munitions workers and customs officials. There were medals for 'blameless service' in the police or the prison guard, medals of 'imperial favour' for individuals whose contributions to hospitals, orphanages, churches and social welfare were brought to the attention of the Tsar. There were medals 'to the useful' and 'for loyal zeal', awarded to the subject peoples of the Russian Empire.

Society Medals

A very large number of medals are awarded by societies and other organisations to individuals for outstanding services. Unlike the majority of the medals and decorations mentioned elsewhere in this book, these medals are either semi-official or unofficial and are therefore seldom worn in uniform, even though they are supplied with suspenders and ribbons in the same way as military medals are. There is no clear-cut dividing line between those medals of certain societies

Grace Darling, the heroine of a famous life-saving feat, was awarded a medal by the Royal Humane Society

below, top row, left The Stanhope Gold Medal which is given every year for the bravest deed of life saving
right The Board of Trade first awarded their Medal for Saving Life in 1854. This one was given in 1936. It has a red ribbon with two white stripes
bottom The War Medal for Bravery at Sea which was given by Lloyds in December 1940. It has a white ribbon with two blue stripes
facing page Other medals awarded by the Royal Humane Society for bravery in saving lives. The society has been awarding medals since 1775

which are occasionally worn, on the opposite breast to all other decorations, and those which are not worn with uniform at all.

The main category of medals awarded by private bodies, which are sometimes permitted on uniform, consists of life-saving medals. In Britain gold, silver and bronze medals are awarded by the Royal National Life-boat Institution for services in saving the lives of shipwrecked seamen. The medals were instituted in 1824 and bore the effigy of the reigning sovereign down to the end of the reign of George V. Since the accession of King George VI in 1936 these medals have portrayed the founder of the institution, Sir William Hillary, since the medals are not awarded by the sovereign. Bars are awarded for further acts of bravery. The Royal Humane Society awards a number of different medals, the most coveted of which is the Stanhope Gold Medal, one of which is awarded each year for the bravest deed of life-saving. The Society also awards silver and bronze medals for rescue in drowning, factory or mining accidents. Other medals are awarded by the Society for the Protection of Life from Fire, the Shipwrecked Fishermen and Mariners Royal Benevolent Society, the Automobile Association and Lloyd's, the famous insurance association.

The corporations of several British cities also make their own awards for bravery, life-saving, police service, ambulance work and special duties in time of war. London, Birmingham, Liverpool and Glasgow are among those whose awards may be encountered. Incidentally awards have been made to British servicemen and civilians by such towns and cities as Kimberley, Hong Kong and Shanghai for services in time of war or other crises.

Certain organisations such as the Red Cross, Boy Scouts and the Girl Guides are to be found all over the world and the medals which they award may range from a purely local medal, at district, county or regional level, to international awards. While many of the national and international medals of the Boy Scouts, for example, are meant to be worn (the Silver Wolf, the Silver Acorn, the Cornwell badge for gallantry and so on) the majority of the medals awarded at the local level are not really intended for wear, even though they may be fitted with a ring or suspension bar. One can make a large and varied collection of medals issued by international organisations, specialising in the awards made by such bodies as Rotary International and Lions Clubs, youth movements such as the Scouts and Guides,

above, top The Meritorious Service Medal was awarded by the Southern Railways. The ribbon is green with yellow rails and sleepers
left A medal awarded by the Royal Welsh Agricultural Society for long service. It has a white-striped red ribbon with central green stripe
right A Long Service Medal awarded by the Royal Agricultural Society of England. It has a red ribbon

Pathfinders, Young Pioneers, Boys Brigades and Girls Guildry. All of them provide examples of medals at local, national and international level.

Different professions, occupations and even hobbies produce numerous examples of medals connected with them and offer scope for a collection of items associated with a particular subject. Those with an interest in farming could collect the medals awarded by the Royal Highland and Agricultural Society in Scotland, the Royal Agricultural Society of England and the Royal Welsh Agricultural Society. Similar bodies are to be found in most countries nowadays and most of them have one thing in common—they have a medal, or medals, awarded annually for services to the club or society, for long service proficiency in farming or outstanding services to agriculture in general.

Institutional medals range enormously from parochial horticultural shows to the Royal Geographical Society, from the Birmingham Lunar Society to the Royal Society itself—Britain's premier learned institution. On the international scene the most coveted medals are those awarded to recipients of the annual Nobel Prizes. With the large gold medals, awarded for Physics, Chemistry, Physiology (Medicine), Literature and Peace, go a diploma and a sum of money which varies between £8,000 and £12,000, the amount being dependent on the income of the Nobel Foundation.

Academic Medals

It is sad to think that many of the so-called medals awarded by schools and colleges have now been commuted into cash awards or prize books. The price of silver and gold, and the costs of engraving and striking medals have soared terrifically since the First World War and have made the production of these medals prohibitive. Conversely the funds which originally endowed these awards have shrunk in true worth as the value of money has fallen over the years.

The late nineteenth century was the heyday of the school prize medal, when almost every school of any size had several of these medals for award to pupils who were outstanding in various subjects. Often these medals were named after the original benefactor whose effigy might even be shown on the obverse. Other subjects depicted might be the school's coat of arms or even a view of the school building itself. The reverse was usually left blank, for the name of the pupil and the date of the award to be engraved. School medals of this sort are now increasing in popularity with collectors. They were often mounted with a ribbon so that they could be worn by their proud recipients. Collectors either concentrate on the medals of one school, or locality, or collect any medal awarded for a particular subject, such as mathematics, science, history or art. School medals awarded to boys and girls who later rose to prominence in national affairs are eagerly sought after as 'association items' by collectors.

An interesting category of school medals are those which were once awarded for perfect or near-perfect attendance. They were awarded at one time (usually before the First World War) to pupils for perfect attendance over a period of at least two years. They bore the name and crest of the school and an inscription such as 'Perfect attendance'. They were suspended by ribbons which usually had a brooch mounting at the top so that they could be pinned to blazer or gymtunic. Continued perfect attendance was recognised by the award of bars inscribed 'One Year', 'Two Years' and so on. These medals were usually in brass, bronze or pewter, more rarely in silver and were a great source of pride and joy to their wearers—and their parents—and many a child who would nowadays be confined to bed would struggle out to school in all weathers and with all ailments in order that the record should not be broken. In certain cases perfect attendance over

longer periods was rewarded by a silver or gold watch, suitably inscribed.

In the category of academic medals come the large number of awards made by colleges, universities and institutions of higher learning, either as prizes or for services in fields of the arts and sciences.

Sports Medals

Many of the medals in this group are similar to those in the last, in that they were awarded by schools and colleges. Here again there is plenty of scope for the collector and it is advisable to concentrate either on the medals awarded by a particular school or the medals connected with a particular sport such as boxing, swimming or athletics. At the international level there are bronze, silver and gold medals awarded in connection with the Olympic Games, the South Pacific Games, the British Empire and Commonwealth Games, the Caribbean Games and other fixtures. The medals awarded in connection with these events are comparatively rare and most of the events are so recent that few awards are likely to be available to the collector as yet. Some collectors specialise in the awards made to particular sportsmen—footballers, boxers, cricketers and champion jockeys among others.

A team of sheep dogs from Wales who have come to compete in an international trial. The greatest honour for a shepherd is to win a medal in such a competition

LEST WE FORGET

FAC-SIMILE OF MEDAL STRUCK BY GERMANY
TO COMMEMORATE THE EVENT
Translation of wording on Medal
BUSINESS ABOVE EVERYTHING   NO CONTRABAND — THE
CUNARD LINE – CUNARD-BOOKING   GREAT LINER LUSITANIA

The Sinking of the Lusitania.
May 7th 1915.

8 COMMEMORATIVE MEDALS

Collectors are often puzzled by large metallic objects which look like coins, yet have no figure of value inscribed on them, or look like medals, yet may not have a ring or bar for suspension. These objects are probably commemorative medals. The term 'medalet' is often used to describe a medal which is smaller than usual, while 'medallion' is sometimes used to describe one which is larger than usual. The term 'medallion' is often, though incorrectly, used by collectors to denote any commemorative medal not intended for wear by the recipient.

This type of medal is actually much older than the others so far described in this book. It had its origins in ancient times. Among the earliest items are the large silver ten-drachmae coins minted by Syracuse in the fifth century B.C. and given as prizes to athletes competing in the Assinarian and

Demareteian Games. Theoretically these beautiful pieces, with their profiles of Arethusa, were money and could be spent, but it is likely that the winners regarded them as prize medals to be carefully cherished. Originally armour captured from the Athenians was given as prizes but eventually this was transformed into these medal-coins, though tiny suits of armour labelled *'athla'* (prizes) were depicted on the coins.

The Romans struck large brass 'coins' which were intended as commemorative medals rather than as actual money. The idea disappeared for over a thousand years, but was revived in fifteenth century Italy by Antonio Pisano, a sculptor who produced an attractive bronze piece portraying the last Byzantine emperor, John VIII Palaeologus, to commemorate his visit to Italy in 1438. This medal, and others produced in Italy in the fifteenth and sixteenth centuries, were cast in moulds from clay originals. This method limited the number of medals which could be produced and therefore these early medals are very rare. In the sixteenth century, when the craze for medals spread to Germany, the Germans began striking medals from engraved dies, in the same way as coins were produced, and this method permitted a greater number of medals in each edition. The Italian medals were beautifully designed, usually bearing a portrait on the obverse and an animal, landscape or symbolic design on the reverse. Medals were produced on behalf of princes and poets, rulers and statesmen, extolling their virtues or commemorating their achievements. In this way the medals of Renaissance Europe came to be miniature pieces of history. The fashion for these medals spread to England in the reign of Henry VIII and several excellent examples dating from that period are preserved in the British Museum in London.

In the seventeenth century commemorative medals took on a new function. In the days before such mass media as newspapers, radio and television, the medal was used to spread a political message. Numerous medals of the seventeenth century satirised unpopular politicians or criticised foreign countries, or bore patriotic slogans and pictures. The struggles between Protestants and Catholics in Britain and the Netherlands are faithfully reproduced in the satirical medals of the period. The defeat of James II and the subsequent struggles between the Jacobites and the supporters of the House of Orange also resulted in a large crop of political medals. Medals were produced not only to commemorate important events

facing page An artist's impression of the sinking of the *Lusitania*, inset is the British forgery of the German medal commemorating the event

Silver medal commemorating the Numismatic Exhibition of 1887. Obverse and reverse

A silver medal commemorating the
Consecration of St. Vladimir in Kiev.
Obverse and reverse

but to reward loyal service and outstanding acts of bravery and devotion to duty. In this way the gallantry awards and campaign medals discussed in earlier chapters had their origins.

In the eighteenth and nineteenth centuries medals were struck by the government, by societies and institutions and by private individuals for all manner of events and purposes. Eventually it became fashionable for many towns and cities to commission a medal to commemorate important local events, such as the inauguration of a new gasworks or the opening of a railway line, or the launching of a ship. A large collection could be formed of these local medals which had their heyday in the mid-nineteenth century.

Commemorative medals gradually went into decline in the early years of the twentieth century, but not before they had a last flowering as a propaganda weapon during the First World War. Medals of this nature were used very effectively by the Germans, either to boost the morale of the civilian populace or to strike fear and terror into the hearts of the enemy, or to win over neutral countries to the German side. Medals were struck to commemorate important victories, to explain the reasons for the submarine campaign against neutral shipping and to threaten what fate would befall the British and French when the war was won. A controversial medal was the so-called Lusitania Medal, said to have been struck to commemorate the sinking of the *Lusitania* by a German submarine in May 1915. The medal was designed by Karl Götz and struck by the Germans to satirise the levity of mind of the Cunard Line, in ignoring warnings by the German government that the *Lusitania* would be treated as an enemy warship if it was used to carry war materials to the Allies. The fact that the Germans would even consider striking a medal for an event which had resulted in the deaths of some 1,198 people was seized on by the British who promptly issued 'copies' of the medal as souvenirs of 'German frightfulness'. The British forgery, which is quite common, has the spelling error MAY instead of the German MAI in the date of the event.

The increasing use of popular newspapers, the cinema and radio in the 1920s led to the decline of the commemorative medal in its popular form. Hitherto no event of national or international importance would have passed without a spate of commemorative medals having been produced in its honour. Compared to the hundreds of different medals produced as souvenirs of the 1911 Coronation, the Silver Jubilee of King George V

(1935) and the Coronation of King George VI (1937) passed almost unnoticed by the purveyors of popular medals. There was a great revival of commemorative medals in the early 1960s and although the Coronation of Queen Elizabeth in 1953 passed almost unnoticed in this respect there were many different medals produced to celebrate the investiture of the Prince of Wales in 1969. Few of the commemorative medals of the present day are mounted with a device for suspension. Unlike so many of their predecessors they are seldom intended to be worn, but are meant to repose in velvet-lined cases and presentation cabinets for the delight of the collector.

There has also been a revival of the nineteenth century habit of producing medals in long sets. This practice began some time earlier when the French medallist Jean Dassier produced sets of medals portraying the 72 rulers of France, from the earliest times to Louis XV and followed this with a series portraying the kings of England from William the Conqueror to George II. Dassier, who hailed from Switzerland, also issued sets of medals portraying Genevan theologians, historical events and celebrities connected with Geneva and crowned his work with a set of 60 Roman emperors. Dassier was emulated in Britain by J. Kirk whose series of portrait medals included royalty, the nobility, members of Parliament and prominent figures of the eighteenth and early nineteenth century. Sir Edward Thomason re-issued the Dassier medals in 1820 and followed this with lengthy sets of his own, including 36 medals featuring the Elgin Marbles, sixteen medals devoted to aspects of the sciences and 60 medals depicting biblical subjects. A. J. Stothard produced a series of Great Men medals. J. Mudie produced a set of 44 medals showing famous battles of the Napoleonic Wars and Moritz Fürst issued 27 medals commemorating battles in the War of 1812 between the United States and Britain. Medallic sets returned to popularity in the 1960s and a number of interesting sets have appeared in the United States, Britain and the countries of Europe in recent years.

The coronation coach on the way to the Abbey carrying Her Majesty Queen Elizabeth II. The troops who lined the route received the Coronation Medal

9 PINS AND BADGES

With the exception of the badges given to veterans of both world wars for service to King and country badges have seldom been used in Britain and the Commonwealth for recognising military services. In many other countries, however, pins and badges are awarded instead of medals, and are worn on uniform jackets and tunics in the same way. They are often of great interest, on account of the circumstances in which they were awarded, and are certainly worthy of collection and study.

The Imperial Russian Army favoured badges either for personal adornment pure and simple or in recognition of long service or special service. Well over a thousand different badges are thought to have been produced. Every regiment and military unit had its own distinctive badges. They were often presented to officers to celebrate the centenary or the jubilee of the foundation of the regiment and were generally designed by the commanding officer. Many of these badges were surprisingly artistic in design, incorporating scenes of battles in which the regiment had distinguished itself. Others included the coats of arms of aristocrats who founded the regiment or served with it. The first of these breast badges is thought to have been instituted in 1827 when they were awarded to the officers of the First Grenadier

Companies of the Preobrazhensky and Seme-novsky Imperial Guard. This badge bore the monogram of Tsar Alexander I and was struck in silver.

These badges increased in popularity through-out the nineteenth century. In addition to the breast badges were smaller badges worn from a chain threaded through the buttonhole of the tunic. They were nearly always made of precious metal and were often beautifully decorated with coloured enamels. In 1912 regimental badges of this kind were awarded to other ranks. Their badges were similar in design to those worn by officers but were usually in bronze or white metal without enamelling. Breast badges were mounted with a brooch so that they could be pinned to the pocket or breast. Others were mounted with a small nut so that they could be screwed on to a special plate attached to the pocket of the uniform or a special slot in the tunic halfway between the collar and the belt. Badges of regiments, military schools and cadet units were worn on the left side of the chest, while those of military academies, military doctors, graduates of officer schools, specialised schools and civilian institutions were worn on the right side.

This practice ceased after the Revolution, but was gradually revived in the 1920s in limited cases. The imperial system of regimental badges was abolished altogether, but badges are still awarded for various purposes. Units of the Red Army which display outstanding service in war-time receive a badge bearing a five-pointed star and a red banner. The badge is worn by all members of the unit, whether they were present at the action for which the award was made or not. Special badges were awarded during the Second World War to civilians who trained in anti-aircraft or chemical warfare defence. Similar badges were given to civilians who served with the Red Cross or the Red Crescent medical services. Other badges which are now awarded include specialist badges, for those who pass service examinations in specialised fields, re-enlistment badges, which are awarded for service of four years and upwards, and the diamond-shaped badge awarded to graduates of Soviet military academies.

The United States has made extensive use of badges for service in the armed forces. A small circular gilt badge is awarded by the Department of Defense to its civilian employees for 'excep-tionally meritorious service within and beyond the call of duty'. This award has no ribbon and is

Russian gold medal commemorating the death of Alexander II in 1881. Obverse

Russian gold medal commemorating the Coronation of Alexander III in 1883. Obverse

Russian Gold medal commemorating the 100th anniversary of the founding of St. George's Cross. The heads of Catherine the Great and Alexander II are shown

pinned directly to the jacket. Small circular badges are similarly awarded to civilians who served with the Army or Air Force for meritorious service.

In February 1942 a system of unit citations was adopted for the Army and Navy of the United States. These citations were awarded to units and ships which served in actions in exceptionally difficult and dangerous conditions. In the first instance the unit or ship was awarded a guidon, or pennant, which thus roughly corresponds to the British Army system of flags embellished with battle honours. For second citations, however, members of the unit or ship were awarded the individual decoration, consisting of a blue ribbon set in a gold-coloured frame of laurel leaves worn above the pocket on the right side of the chest.

Map showing the path of the *Nautilus* on her historic voyage
OFFICIAL U.S. NAVY PHOTOGRAPH

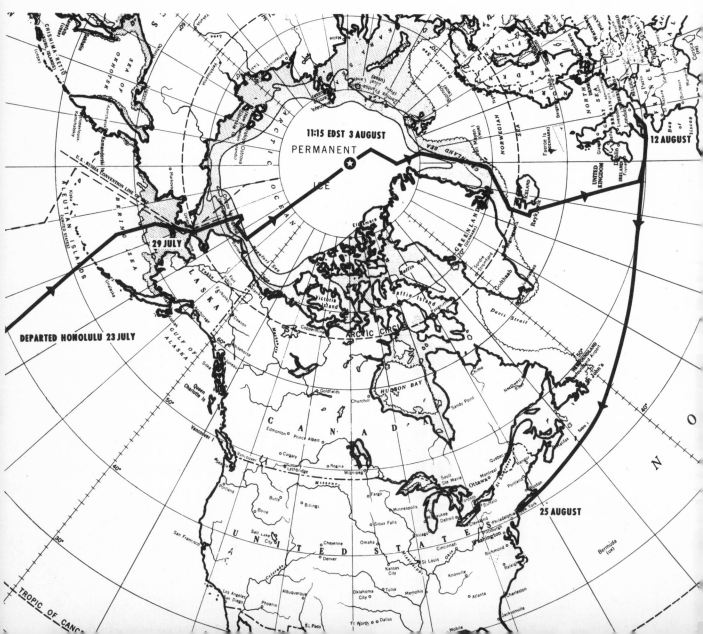

For each subsequent occasion an oak leaf cluster is added to the decoration. Officers and men who were serving with the unit when the citation was awarded are permitted to wear it permanently, even though they subsequently transfer to another unit. Officers and men who join the unit after the award are permitted to wear the individual decoration for the period in which they serve with the unit. The individual decoration worn by sailors has three horizontal stripes of blue, scarlet and gold. Bronze citation stars are worn on the gold part of the ribbon. An interesting exception to this was the individual decoration awarded to members of the crew of the nuclear submarine *Nautilus* in 1958 after it successfully sailed from the Pacific to the Atlantic under the Polar ice. The ribbon was worn with a special gold 'N'.

USS *Nautilus* at anchor in Pearl Harbour before her history-making journey under the North Pole to England

The Nazi Pilots' and Observers' Joint Badge which was awarded to those who had qualified for both badges

Reichsfuhrer SS Himmler talking to an SS Gruppenfuhrer (right). They are both wearing breast badges. *right* The Marchese Marconi wearing the buttonhole rosette of the Grand Cross of the Royal Victorian Order

above right The Nazi Blockade Runner's Award. This was given to crews of ships that reached port after declaration of war or were sunk or scuttled to evade capture
above The two designs of cap badge for the S.S. or *Schutzstaffeln*. The later design is on the right

Other American badges awarded in connection with the Second World War include the Honourable Discharge emblem, awarded to veterans of the armed forces, and the Gold Star, awarded to the mothers of servicemen killed in action.

Nazi Germany had a number of badges which could be worn in uniform. The most important of these was the Gold Party Badge, awarded to those who belonged to the Nazi Party before it came to power in January 1933. It consisted of a black swastika on a white enamelled circle surrounded by an inscription on a red background and gold laurel leaves. Wound badges were awarded to servicemen wounded in action and correspond to the American Purple Heart. They had no medal ribbons and were pinned directly to the pocket. The badges were oval in shape and were issued in different types of metal: black metal for one or two wounds, in silver for three or four wounds, and in gold for five or more. The Army badge featured crossed swords surmounted by a steel helmet bearing a swastika, while the naval badge had crossed swords superimposed on an anchor, the whole surrounded by an anchor cable.

Among the more recent badges awarded for special services may be mentioned the Jerusalem Defence Badge (*Magen Yerushalaim*) awarded to Jewish soldiers who took part in the defence of Jerusalem during the war of June 1948. The badge, pinned to the left pocket, consists of a bronze shield with a sword and spray of laurel in white metal. Every soldier who belonged to the Palmach military organisation before the end of November 1947 was awarded the Palmach Badge, featuring two ears of corn and a sword. A similar badge was awarded to members of the Jewish Brigade Group and since then other badges have been produced in recognition of service in other formations and later campaigns.

Badges in bronze, white metal or enamelled metal are awarded to soldiers in many European armies for proficiency in shooting, long service and good conduct and are too numerous to mention in detail. Like the badges of Tsarist Russia many of them incorporate regimental insignia and are attractive additions to any collection of military awards.

**Cap badges of
British Army regiments**

left to right, this page, top row
17th/21st Lancers
The Leicestershire Regiments
middle row
The Welsh Guards
The Royal Scots Greys
The Seaforth Highlanders

facing page, top row
the 10th Royal Hussars
the Royal Regiment of Artillery
middle row
The Argyll and Sutherland Highlanders
The 11th Hussars
bottom row
The Suffolk Regiment
The Queen's Bays
The Buffs

The Grenadier Guards going off duty during the Changing of the Guard Ceremony

A gun crew of the Royal Horse Artillery firing a salute in St James's Park

10 MEDAL RIBBONS AND EMBELLISHMENTS

The pieces of coloured ribbon by which medals are suspended are commonly worn on their own nowadays, on all but ceremonial occasions. With practice you can learn to recognise the different colours and combinations and take in at a glance the career of a soldier, sailor or airman by the ribbons on his chest. Medal ribbons are today's equivalent of the standards, guidons and decorated shields of medieval knights. The order in which ribbons are worn is more or less the same for all countries: decorations and orders first, followed by campaign medals, followed by medals for long service and efficiency, followed by medals awarded by foreign countries, in the order in which they were given. The majority of British medal ribbons are $1\frac{1}{4}$ inches wide. The ribbons of the United Nations Medal for Korea, the Victoria Cross, George Cross, the Order of the Bath and most other orders and decorations are $1\frac{1}{2}$ inches wide. The ribbon of the Order of Merit, which has only recently been permitted to be worn on its own, is 2 inches wide. The ribbons of the orders of the Garter, Thistle and St. Patrick are 4 inches wide, but are never worn on their own. Conversely the only smaller ribbon is that worn with the medals for Long and Faithful Service to King George V or King George VI, which is $1\frac{1}{8}$ inches wide and is something of a curiosity since it has broad royal blue diagonal stripes descending from left to right, flanked by vertical crimson bars. The ribbon worn with Queen Victoria's Faithful Service Medal was even narrower, but was never intended for wear on its own. This ribbon had horizontal stripes of yellow and white on top of a patch of ribbon in the Royal Stewart tartan. This curious medal was given to members of the Royal Household after 25 years personal service to the Queen.

Most foreign medals and decorations have rather wider ribbons than Britain, usually of $1\frac{1}{2}$ inches or more. One of the few American exceptions is the ribbon of the Medal of Honor which is a ribbon little more than an inch wide. Both Germany and Russia, on the other hand, have favoured narrower ribbons, of an inch or even less in some cases. This narrower style is more suitable for the curious pentagonal method of mounting the ribbons with the medals. Imperial Austrian medals were also mounted in an unusual manner, in such a way that the ribbon had a triangular appearance with the point at the lower, or medal, end.

Both Germany and Russia tended to favour the same medal ribbons with many different awards. Thus it would have been very difficult to tell much about the career of a German or Russian soldier merely from the ribbons on his chest, had they been worn on their own. As a rule, however, medals were worn in full. In a few cases Britain used the same ribbon on several occasions. The red, white, yellow and blue ribbon of watered silk was used for the Jellalabad Medal of 1842, the India Medals of 1842–43 and the Kabul-Kandahar Star of 1880. The China Medals of 1857–60 and 1900 had similar ribbons while the ribbons of the Distinguished Service Order and the Military General Service Medal are not dissimilar. The ribbon of Commander of the Order of the Bath is virtually the same as that of the Victoria Cross, but confusion is avoided by the tiny cross worn on the VC ribbon.

Most medal ribbons are either of one colour all over, or have vertical stripes or bars of different colours. In a few cases the contrasting stripes are diagonal—a style adopted in 1918 by Britain for the RAF decorations and subsequently followed by Greece and the Netherlands for their air force decorations. Diagonal stripes may also be found on the ribbon of the French medal for Deportees and the Long and Faithful Service medals for the British Royal Household. The Belgian medal for Deportees has a curious V-shaped pattern of narrow stripes in the Belgian national colours. Several ribbons have horizontal stripes—the

Alexander II reorganized the classes of the Cross
of St George during the Crimean War. There
were various privileges attached to winning one

ALEXANDER II.

EMPEROR OF RUSSIA.

Queen Victoria on one of her favourite ponies
with John Brown holding its head. He was
awarded her Faithful Service Medal which has
the most curious ribbon of any British Medal

American Merchant Marine Combat Bar, the Belgian Political Prisoners Medal of 1914–18 and the French campaign medal for service in Madagascar.

Medal ribbons are often embellished with tiny ornaments. These are either miniature versions of palms, oak-leaves and clusters which are worn on the ribbon with the medal itself, or consist of rosettes or stars which indicate that the wearer holds bars or clasps to the medal itself. Silver rosettes on the ribbons of the British 1939–45 campaign stars indicate that bars for subsequent campaigns have been awarded. Similar rosettes on the ribbons of decorations, such as the DSO, the MC and the MM denote that the recipient was awarded bars to the original decoration. A gold rosette on the ribbon of a decoration indicates that the recipient has four bars to the decoration. A similar system, using tiny five-pointed stars, is used in the United States.

Replicas of the decorations are sometimes worn on the ribbon, when the full decoration is not being worn. As well as the miniature bronze cross worn on the VC ribbon, there is a tiny silver cross worn on the George Cross ribbon. Officers of the American Legion of Merit wear a gold miniature of the badge on their ribbons. Second awards of the American Medal of Honor are denoted by a bronze oak-leaf cluster (Army) or a gold star (Navy). The different palms and stars found on the ribbon of the French *Croix de Guerre* have already been mentioned in Chapter 4. German servicemen who won the Iron Cross in both world wars were given a tiny eagle and swastika emblem with the date 1939 for wear on the ribbon of their original cross.

Many European decorations have tiny crossed swords which are worn on the ribbon to indicate that the holder has been awarded the military version of the decoration. Circular rosettes covered with ribbon, or small bows, are often found on Continental decorations. Until recently these Continental devices were worn on the ribbon of the Royal Victorian Order when this decoration had been awarded to a foreigner, but this practice has now been dropped. These bows and ribbon rosettes are also worn by their recipients as a button-hole decoration when in civilian dress.

Military outfitters usually carry a large stock of medal ribbons, going right back to the Napoleonic Wars, so that recipients of medals and decorations can purchase fresh ribbon when required, or to enable collectors to get the right ribbon to go with the items in their collections. There is some controversy, however, regarding the replacement of medal ribbons. Some collectors maintain that the ribbon which was actually worn by the recipient is preferable to a brand new ribbon, even though the original ribbon may be faded and frayed at the edges. Most collectors feel that the original ribbon is of no particular significance and prefer to enhance the appearance of their medals by mounting them with nice, clean ribbon. Medal ribbons are sold for a few pence an inch. A very attractive collection of medal ribbons can be formed at a reasonable outlay. When cut and sewn up into strips of the proper depth they can be mounted on sheets of white card and the details of the medal and its dates neatly printed above. This is a good substitute—until such time as the actual medals themselves can be bought or otherwise acquired.

11 COLLECTING MEDALS AND DECORATIONS

There are various ways of approaching medal-collecting. Many collectors become interested in the hobby by inheriting the medals of a friend or relative. It may only be the First World War trio, or a small group of Second World War campaign stars and the War Medal, but it is enough to start the collection. With a small nucleus of this sort you may decide to collect any medal that comes your way, both British and foreign, both civil and military. Pawnbrokers' shops, junk shops and street barrows used to be the happy hunting ground of the general collector and many rare items could be picked up for little more than their scrap value. Now this has all changed and the days when pairs of the Queen's and King's South African Medals could be bought for less than a pound, and 1939–45 campaign stars rated only a few pence, are now over. Thousands of Nazi medals and decorations were brought back to Britain or America by servicemen after the war and at one time were a glut on the market. Now there is such a demand for them that they have even been forged!

All this is due to the fact that medal-collecting has grown rapidly as a hobby. The law of supply and demand is now in operation, and therefore few beginners can afford to collect haphazardly. It is best to decide at the outset what you are going to collect, and then stick to this plan. In this way you will save yourself a great deal of expense. Unless you decide to form a straightforward collection, with one example of each medal within a certain period (from the Boer War to the present day, for example) you will be confronted with medals in groups. You may purchase the Boer War pair and then subsequently be offered a four-medal group consisting of the Queen's South African Medal and the three First World War Medals. Either you turn down the second purchase, or you end up with two examples of the Queen's South African Medal. At one time beginners would have been tempted to buy the second group and remove the Queen's South African Medal from it, for sale or exchange to another collector. This is nothing short of vandalism—unfair to the memory of the man who originally won the medals and, apart from anything else, likely to affect the value of the group, if and when you yourself come to sell it. All too often in the past groups were split up by dealers who had a customer for the rare items and, as a result many collectors of the present day spend many fruitless hours searching through dealers' stocks in the hunt for missing items to make up these broken groups. This applies particularly in cases where a soldier was awarded a decoration, such as the DCM or the Military Medal, in addition to his campaign medals. You will often find gallantry awards sold on their own, and the hunt then begins for the missing campaign medals. The latter may not have been highly regarded by the dealer who originally handled the group, but collectors like to have the various medals which add background and interest to gallantry awards.

After a time most collectors prefer to specialise in a certain field. You could collect medals and decorations of soldiers belonging to the local regiment. With luck these are the medals which should be most readily available in your locality anyway. A visit to your local regimental museum is useful, not only because it will have a fine display of the medals for which the regiment was eligible, but also because it will house the regimental records, muster rolls and medal rolls which provide so much of the background story to those medals in your collection.

Alternatively you may like to collect medals awarded to sailors of the Royal Navy or the Merchant Marine, ranging from the Naval General Service Medal of Napoleonic times up to the Atlantic Star and the general service awards since the Second World War. Another form of semi-specialised collecting is to study the medals awarded for service in certain areas, in India or Africa for example. Specialist collectors narrow the field considerably, and may concentrate on getting hold of examples of the Naval General Service Medal awarded to a seaman from each of the ships which took part in the Battle of Trafalgar, or examples of the Waterloo Medal named to members of each regiment and formation present on that occasion.

Housing the Collection

Medals present a number of problems with regard to their storage and mounting. Wall cases and cabinets with shallow drawers are available, but these are bulky and also very expensive. The beginner or collector of modest means usually has to make do with something less elaborate. Shirt boxes, or any cardboard box which is about 12 inches wide, 18 inches long and just over an inch deep, are ideal for housing a medal collection. Pieces of wood or hardboard can be cut just slightly smaller than the inside of the box and covered with green baize or some similar material. The medals can be laid out neatly in rows on the baize and held in place by brass drawing pins stuck through the underside of the ribbon, at top and bottom. Small cards, with the name, rank, regiment and number of the recipient, where known, can be mounted on the board above each medal or group. These boxes are best stored in an upright position, so that the weight of other boxes on top does not cause any harm to the box of medals at the foot of the pile.

Groups of medals may be kept together, with the medals slightly overlapping, as originally worn by the recipient. Many collectors, however, prefer to dismount the medals from the original brooch mounting and lay them out on boards, so that the detail of each medal can clearly be seen. Moreover, this method prevents damage from one medal rubbing against another.

Care and Condition of Medals

Collectors use certain terms to describe the condition of medals, in the same way as coin collectors describe their coins. These terms are also used in dealer's price-lists and auctioneers' catalogues, so it is important to know what they mean. Extremely Fine (EF) denotes a medal which is in brilliant condition, with no scratches or signs of wear. Very Fine (VF) describes a medal which has obviously been worn, but is nevertheless in splendid condition, with little surface marking. Fine (F) means that the medal has obvious signs of wear, but is still presentable, if no better specimens are available. Very Good (VG) is a term which has been so abused that it now means almost the opposite. A medal in this condition would be well worn, and probably showing dents in its rim as well. A medal in Very Good condition would only be worth having if it was a very rare item, with unusual or rare bars.

In modern times there are so very few occasions when servicemen would have the opportunity to wear their medals that the vast majority of medals from 1918 onwards tend to be found in EF or VF condition. Many of the Second World War medals, awarded to ex-servicemen after they were demobilised, may never have been worn at all. They are frequently found in the original cardboard box, the recipients never having taken the trouble to mount them into groups.

Before the First World War, however, the wearing of medals was customary on all but the most informal occasions and when actually serving on active duty. Thus medals could be, and often were, subject to a great deal of wear. It will be found that the reverse side of these medals is usually considerably more worn than the obverse (or upper) side, on account of the constant rubbing against the tunic. Medals worn by cavalrymen are often found in poor condition, with scratches and edge knocks caused by the constant jangling on horseback. Often the medals in a group have an abrasive effect on each other. For this reason the Queen's Medal for Egypt (1881) is comparatively rare in excellent condition, since it was usually worn next to the Khedive's Star whose points were capable of doing considerable damage. Apart from these factors it should be remembered that part of the ritual of 'spit and polish' involved one's medals and they were often submitted to vigorous cleaning with metal polish. Dirty medals may be cleaned by gentle immersion in warm soapy water and light brushing with a soft silver brush. But metal polish should *never* be brought anywhere near your medals!

Dealers often sell medals 'as worn', a euphemism which conceals a lifetime of hardy service on the chest of some grizzled veteran. But because of the strong personal element involved in medal-collecting, genuine wear does not affect the value of a medal to the same degree as it would the value of a coin. There are many collectors who feel that such signs of wear enhance the interest and value of a medal, and for the same reason they prefer to keep the original medal ribbons, even though they may be faded and threadbare.

Medals have sometimes been put to uses other than those for which they were produced and consequently bear the marks of their conversion. They be found with pin and clasp mounts converting them into brooches. They may be found with silver 'feet' and brackets transforming them into menu stands (a favourite device at one time). Such converted medals are of little value to collectors, but occasionally unscrupulous dealers attempt to convert them back to their original condition. Be on your guard against medals with solder marks, or filing marks. These signs indicate that the medal has either been reconverted or, worse still, faked by the addition or substitution of engagement bars. It seems a pity to end on a note of warning, but I would most strongly advise you to purchase medals only from established and reputable dealers, and always be suspicious if a 'bargain' is offered.

Pipe Major J. Jenkinson of the Black Watch Regiment

INDEX